French Flea Bites

George East

Illustrations by Robin Evans

French Flea Bites

Published by
La Puce Publications
87 Laburnum Grove
North End
Portsmouth PO2 0HG

Telephone: 023 92 678148
Facsimile: 023 92 665070

© George East 2000

This paperback edition 2000

ISBN 0 9523635 3 4

The author asserts the moral right to
be identified as the author of this work

Designed and typeset by Nigel at Christianson Hoper Norman
Reprographics by SP Digital
Printed in Great Britain by Borcombe Printers PLC Hampshire

Author's Note

This is the fourth book in what was originally meant to be a series of one.

When my wife insisted I write a follow-up to *Home & Dry in France*, I protested that I'd said everything there was to say about living in our quiet corner of Normandy.

Three books on, and there is still no shortage of fodder for my scribblings, as increasingly peculiar situations develop and what many people would call weird characters wander mostly uninvited into our lives.

During a recent trip across the Channel, a woman asked me how I managed to dream up all the obviously fictional people and bizarre events in my books. She then went on to solemnly describe how she and her husband had completely demolished a mud and straw wall of their cottage in the Auvergne in the belief they were merely stripping off layer after layer of traditional French flock wallpaper.

After all these years and encounters, it seems to me that (to put it politely) the most unusual people choose to make their lives in every region of our adopted country, and especially in our direct vicinity. My wife says it is me, and that I act as a magnet for unusual people and circumstances.

Whether or not this is so, most of the stories in the following pages happened more or less as I describe them, allowing for a little artistic licence and the avoidance of embarrassment; anyway, truth is, as someone said, more a matter of observation and perception than simple fact.

for my father

Other acknowledgements

As ever, thanks are due to all the people who helped move this latest episode in the La Puce saga from thought to page.

Quite apart from everyone involved in the technical processes, there are the friends all over France who weighed in with their stories and recipes. Then there are all the others who unwittingly contributed by simply passing through our lives, and who make up the real, composite and imaginary characters in these pages.

It should go without saying that my deepest gratitude is reserved for everyone who bothers to read my work, and especially those who actually think enough of it to pay the asking price.

I end this salutation with a small request to all those of you who have paid the admission fee to join us in our adventuring. To help keep our pot boiling and the denizens of La Puce regularly fed, *please* don't lend your copy of this book to anyone else.

I had a letter recently from a nice lady in Huddersfield who proudly told me she has so far added to (as she put it) the La Puce Fan Club by circulating her copies of my books to no fewer than one hundred and forty-eight friends and acquaintances. She is now thinking about going to computer evening classes so she can learn how to put my books on the world wide web and share them with millions.

Thanks a bomb, Hilda.

The story so far

Following a series of disastrous financial excursions, failed publican, private detective and pickled onion manufacturer George East fled with his wife Donella to Normandy.

Settling in a ruined water mill, the couple survived a series of small adventures and doomed schemes to make a living from the Mill of the Flea and its ten acres of fields, woodland, waterways and mud.

The ancient area of the Cotentin occupies most of the Cherbourg peninsula, which is part of Lower Normandy. A land of rolling landscapes, rugged coastlines and fiercely independent people, this part of northern France can be a place of magic to those who take the time to discover its charms.

The village of Néhou has one shop, a garage, a church and a population of around three hundred. It is as like and unlike any other small rural community as it is possible to imagine, or you wish to make it.

C'est une étrange entreprise que celle de faire rire les honnêtes gens.
(It's an odd job, making decent people laugh.)

La Critique de l'école des femmes (1663)

Prologue

I t is a very special moment for my wife and I and the Mill of the Flea, and good to know the world is joining in our modest celebrations.

Across the planet, night will turn into day as billions of people forget their differences for a few precious moments and millions of clocks strike their own midnight hour. All too soon, the cold light of reality will dawn upon an imperfect world, but for a fleeting heartbeat of time, much of the human race will consider what might have been were we able to see things from each other's eyes.

For the rest of humanity, the celebrations will signal the start of a new millennium. For us, it will be ten years since we stumbled across La Puce.

In truth, it will be nine and a bit years since we first arrived here, but it seems churlish to split hairs on such an opportunity to share this explosion of joy and hope with all mankind.

*　　*　　*　　*　　*

Swaddled against the sharp night air, my wife and I are sitting in front of the caravan, contemplating the wine-dark surface of the big pond. It is almost midnight and hardly a creature is stirring.
Beneath the placid surface, a whole world in microcosm reflects the diversity, dangers and injustices above, but even the constantly warring inmates of our stew pond seem to have called a truce to

hostilities. Perhaps the frogs will even set up a game of football with the crayfish gang to reflect the temporary spirit of universal peace and goodwill.

Around the pond, a string of hurricane lamps send dancing shadows across the water meadow as the capricious Norman wind plays idly with the waist-high grass. A bough creaks as the giant beech trees lining Hunter's Walk nod in approval at the tranquil scene, and the odd grunt, snuffle and hoot shows that many unseen residents are determined not to miss the historic moment.

Reaching for another bacon sandwich, I reflect on the dying year and how the past decade has treated us and our friends and neighbours in the tiny community of Néhou. So much has happened, yet the years have sped by as we have encountered joy, frustration, farce and the occasional tragedy.

Less than a mile away across the tree-lined patchwork of fields, a huddle of houses cling together in the shadow of a sturdy stone church. All over France there are thousands of such villages, all with their own small tales of loss and triumph, greed, envy and kindness to tell. As the rest of the world goes about its business, each will be at the centre of its own universe, with its own community of young and old making their way through life. Every village will have its own René Ribet, Madame Ghislaine and perhaps even its own Jolly Boys Club, where old men meet to put each other and the world to rights.

Having said all that, I cannot believe there is anywhere else on earth quite like St Georges de Néhou.

*   *   *   *   *

As we wait for the big moment, I consider how our friends will be seeing in the new millennium.

During the past months, the subject of how to mark the passing of a thousand years has been the centre of much debate at Jolly

Boys Club meetings. One adventurous member of our unofficial council pressed for a special dinner in the village hall, with the theme of a gastronomic trip around the world to celebrate the diversity of cuisine across the planet. The motion was defeated when nobody could think of any dishes outside France worthy of the effort.

Other unsuccessful proposals included a medieval bingo night and a pageant portraying world events occurring at Néhou, while Old Pierrot's offer of a marathon session retelling his memories of the last century and beyond was turned down out of hand. Although nobody seems to know exactly where, our oldest member lives somewhere outside the village with his various winged and feathered familiars, and claims to be immortal. He once told me that he was blessed and cursed with eternal life by mistakenly drinking from the Holy Grail during a long session with a Crusader who had stopped off for a run ashore at the Cotentin port of Barfleur on his way back from the Holy Lands. Whether or not he will live for ever, our resident mystic has certainly clocked up a good few years, and is known as Old Pierrot to distinguish him from Young Pierrot, another local who is at least eighty.

Our final sub-committee meeting broke up in disarray after René Ribet's apparently serious proposal to mark the date by converting the huge silage clamp at a nearby farm into Néhou's own Millennium Dome and charging gullible visitors to look at it. Everyone in Europe knew the idea had been a total failure in England, my friend the Fox said, but we would obviously make a much better job of it.

Eventually and to everyone's satisfaction, it was decided to mark the occasion by doing absolutely nothing. This, it was felt, would demonstrate to the world (and in particular to our rival village on the other side of the crossroads) that while the passing of a thousand years might be seen as a momentous event in some quarters, to the people of Néhou it is no big deal.

*　　*　　*　　*　　*

According to my wife's new watch, midnight is upon us. In this isolated part of the countryside, there are no signs that others are celebrating the approach of the millennium, and I am not sure that we are in accord with the rest of our time zone as I bought the watch from Dodgy Didier, our local and very general dealer. But in the Cotentin, time is elastic, so the exact moment to start the La Puce firework display is far from critical, and everything else is ready.

I have already rescued the bottle of vintage Normandy champagne from where it has been cooling in the depths of the big pond and filled our earthenware mugs. The handwritten label on the bottle says it was pressed more than a year ago, and this is a long time for fine cider to last in our neck of the woods.

As the big moment approaches, we make our way to the old wooden jetty and I unveil my surprise. Placing the empty cider bottle on one of the few remaining planks, I put a rocket in the neck and light the fuse. I did not buy the rocket from Didier, so am fairly confident it will do its duty.

After a few tense seconds, the glow becomes a shower of sparks and the rocket lifts off, cleaving the night air to join a sea of stars above. It bursts in an explosion of colour as we drink to the new year, century and millennium. Elsewhere, humanity is thronging to share this unique moment, but my wife and I are content to be here, thinking of the good and bad times we have shared while looking after La Puce for a brief moment of its long history.

Through no careful plan or design save that of fate, we have made our life here at Néhou and the Mill of the Flea, and regardless of what has been and what is to come, we both feel we have won at least a small prize in the lottery of life.

A Bite on the Side

All animals are equal, but some animals are more equal than others.

George Orwell, *Animal Farm*

The new millennium has bedded in, and all is *normale* at the Mill of the Flea.

It is raining even inside the mill cottage, yet this morning I found myself up to the knees in the big pond, re-thatching a muskrat's roof.

We are in the midst of a frosty January, and the local soothsayers are predicting an exceptionally hard winter, which will be even harder than last year's exceptionally hard winter, and the one before.

With his usual grim relish, Old Pierrot is also claiming his raven familiar told him we have the mother of all storms waiting in the wings. Consequently, Donella has become even more concerned about the continuing welfare of our non-paying animal guests, so today I was sent off to supplement the diet of a beast which threatens to eat us out of house and home. He is also eating his fellow residents at an alarming rate.

Although the beast has been with us since last summer, today was the first time we have actually had eye-to-eye contact. Usually, the evidence of his presence is limited to the odd splash or occasional sightings of a menacing wake.

Muskrats first appeared in Europe in the early part of this century, and they are as welcome on waterways round here as a rib of English beef in a butcher's shop.

Having moved in, the creature immediately set about creating a series of tunnels and boltholes which would have been the envy of the Colditz escape committee. This has made our big pond even bigger, and his additional network of open ditches makes walking round the water's edge a risky business. Since his arrival, life has also become considerably risky for many of our other residents.

Thanks to his voracious appetite, the cray gang has been decimated, Psycho the goldfish's tribe is down to about half its original number, and our colony of edible frogs have proved extremely edible to the new boss of the big pond.

In spite of all the obvious evidence, Donella has convinced herself that the creature is strictly vegetarian, pointing out the cropped grass ringing his lair. I have tried to explain that the monstrous muskrat is only using the reeds and sedge grass as housing materials, but she will not let me make any movement against him. His daily feeding routine is to slip out from his den and down the bank, then cruise below the surface, leaving a v-shaped trail like a miniature submarine. When he has hoovered up any unwary swimmers, he will make for the nearest of the trenches concealed in the long grass at the waterside, and from there back home. Because of his attentions, the big pond is beginning to look like a rain-filled shell crater, and by the end of last summer there was a somehow disquieting silence in an area once ringing with the croaks, quacks, squeaks and beeps of a whole variety of tenants.

Quite apart from those species actually eaten by him, our other predatory inmates are suffering, and the resident heron is looking positively skeletal. He flapped mournfully overhead this morning, and I could almost count his ribs.

As far as I can tell from my natural history books, our unwanted guest is much bigger than he should be. The nuclear waste recycling station is not far away, so perhaps it is responsible for some sort of dreadful mutation.

Ironically, the purpose of my visit this morning was to supply the overfed muskrat with an expensive supplement to his diet. Donella had found some hamster treat sticks in a local supermarket, and my explicit instructions were to leave the offerings at his front door. In her absence, I tried lobbing the sticks in the general direction of his home from a safe distance. Emboldened by the lack of response, I moved closer and discovering yet another new trench, fell over and plunged my hand through the latticework of reeds and grass which covers the entrance to his den.

Immediately, there was a flurry of activity, an outraged howl, and the thing sank his teeth into my thumb as we came face to face for a heart-stopping instant. In spite of the attack, I am more frightened of my wife than any wild beast, and so was to be found, a grown man with three GCE school certificates and a working knowledge of how to plot longitude, repairing the home of a creature which is turning my beautiful pond into a wasteland.

Far worse than my discomfort is the fact that the giant muskrat has now tasted human blood, and I fear for the safety of the local children who regularly sneak on to our land to fish for Trevor, the lone and now, I believe, entirely legendary trout.

*   *   *   *   *

On my way back to the cottage, I rested at the grotto while staunching the flow of blood from my thumb with a cigarette paper and thinking about our life here at the Mill of the Flea.

Although the time has flashed by, it has been almost a decade since we first arrived at the derelict roadside farmhouse. When we half-heartedly pulled up outside during a house-hunting trip, I didn't think it worth getting out of the car to look at yet another derelict property, but my wife must have somehow scented the hidden treasure that lay beyond.

After our agent had shown us the three walls and half a roof and pointed out the benefits of being able to install double glazing immediately in the holes where once there had been windows, Donella walked to the back of the building and discovered that there was much more to La Puce than at first met the eye.

Along with an equally distressed mill cottage nestling in the dell overlooked by the farmhouse, there were at least ten acres of water meadows, streams and woodland. And there was a ruined bread oven, and an even more ruined well. The Flea, my wife said excitedly, was full of potential and available for no more than the price of a second-hand car. As we discovered during the coming years, the eventual cost of realising that potential could have bought and restored a vintage Rolls Royce. Nevertheless, I am more than content that chance brought us here.

Our years at La Puce have taught me much about life in the countryside anywhere, and the Norman countryside in particular. I have learned about the unchanging nature of the people and why they are as they are, the rhythm of the seasons, the inevitability of the eternal cycle of life and death, the real redness of the tooth and claw of nature, and why one should never try to use a chainsaw while balancing on a stepladder.

*   *   *   *   *

An ill omen this morning when I arrived to serve breakfast at the big pond, and found a frog sitting on the keel of our defunct dinghy, the *Water Flea*. This would not be unusual in summertime, as the upturned boat is a favourite launching pad for Triple Salco and his acrobatic display team. There is nothing stiller than a frog waiting to leap upon a passing snack, as hundreds of dragonflies find to their cost each season, but even our frogs retire for the winter.

There was, however, something unnaturally still about this small creature, and when I reached slowly out to stroke his back, I realised he was frozen solid. Perhaps he had just got his seasonal clock wrong, or perhaps he had bravely sacrificed himself on behalf of his fellows by acting as a lookout for the muskrat. Preferring to believe the latter, I dug a small hole beside the *Water Flea*, and buried the sad remains with full military honours.

I also covered the spot with a huge marble slab spirited away from the undertaker's yard at Bricquebec some years ago. It will be a fitting memorial, and will also hopefully deprive the muskrat of a conveniently ready-frozen meal.

* * * * *

Old Pierrot's raven was right about the storm, and we have had a night to remember.

The rest of France had its own *grande tempête* last month, with seventy people dead and an estimated ten thousand trees laid low by winds of more than a hundred miles an hour.

According to all unbiased reports the country coped magnificently, and when the phone lines were restored, a friend called from the Limousin to demonstrate that it is not only the English who demonstrate a flair for grim humour in the face of adversity. His picture-postcard village of The Three Cherry Trees suffered particularly badly, and has been renamed by the local version of the Jolly Boys Club. It is now known as *Pas Un Seul Cerisier*, or No Cherry Trees At All. There has also been a proposal to show solidarity with a town in England which suffered a similar fate in 1987, and twin No Cherry Trees with One Oak in Kent.

It is heartening to think how natural disasters can bring people together where artificial creations like the EEC have failed so patently to kindle a real sense of international fellowship.

Our storm was a much milder version of the national disaster, but it has left its mark upon the neighbourhood and La Puce. The Cotentin wind is notorious, which is where the tradition of a *bocage* of trees rather than fences or low hedges around fields originates. On the night, we had even more than a particularly stiff blow, and Old Pierrot will doubtless claim it was the Norse gods showing they have not forgotten us.

According to our most senior resident and Scandinavian legend, stormy nights are caused by Helquin the Huntsman, who leads his battalions from Hell across the night skies, with the grim army carrying coffins upon which ride the ghosts of the damned, all filling the air with their pitiful cries of terror and remorse.

In our respectable commune we were of course safe from judgement, but I'm not sure how the miscreants in our rival village of St Jacques de Néhou will have fared.

We had no official warning of what was to come, but the day before the big blow was peculiarly still, and there was not a breath of wind when we made our daily tour to collect firewood from the roadside copse of beech and oak trees.

Arriving at Néhou for a mid-morning coffee break, we saw that most houses had not opened their shutters to greet the day, and the assortment of familiar tractors, mopeds and old cars outside our combined bar and grocery shop showed that the Jolly Boys Club was in extraordinary session.

Inside, we found our friends earnestly discussing not if Old Pierrot's storm would arrive, but how much damage would be done, and what the tree count would be. This was not so much out of concern for the likely level of environmental damage, but in anticipation of the benefits any windfall of free firewood would bring, particularly to those with absentee landlords as neighbours.

Inevitably, Dodgy Didier had set up a book on the total loss of mature trees over the coming twenty four hours, and betting was brisk on the sweepstake covering every parcel of land from the wooded hectares of our local *château* to the smallest back garden with a tree. It was with mixed feelings I learned that the predicted damage at La Puce was low. As Didier explained, our land lies in a hollow, and besides, such has been our neglect of the property that any weak trees have already fallen over of their own accord.

Knowing that the official weather forecasters were predicting a cold, clear and virtually windless night, I reminded the gathering that France was supposed to be a land of logic and science, and took a side bet that there would be no storm.

It was not until we returned to the car that I found my wife had slipped through the curtain between Madame Ghislaine's bar and grocery departments and bought a supply of candles, lantern oil and emergency supplies for our non-paying residents.

By ten o'clock I had the stove on full throttle and was still scoffing at the predictions of a storm, while Donella was making her tour of night-time feeding stations and battening down the garden sheds, log pile and even her favourite cement mixer.

An hour later and the *tempête* had announced its arrival and I had lost my bet. Without warning, the wind had begun to howl in demented fury, banging the shutters and sending tiles skimming off the roof and smashing on to the terrace.

Next, a solid curtain of rain came crashing down, and the waterways on both sides of the cottage started to boil and rage. Looking nervously through the window, I could see that the levels were beginning to rise alarmingly as our tiny home threatened to become an island. We have always felt safe in the wettest of seasons, as the water running by either side of the cottage is its best defence against flooding. The terrain surrounding the mill was painstakingly designed and landscaped to ensure that the power-giving tons of water were guided over the wheel and away under the bridge at great speed, but now it appeared that even the experienced designers of the Mill of the Flea had not anticipated or allowed for this level of downpour.

By midnight, we were making preparations to abandon the cottage and spend the night in the farmhouse safely up on the road when my wife said she could hear the mill wheel creaking even above the roar of the water and the tumult of the rain. This was a strange development, as the huge oaken bucket-wheel was looted soon after the mill fell into disuse at the turn of the last century.

Reluctantly, I put on my waterproofs and went out to investigate, keeping a watchful weather eye out for any passing armies from Hell. Peering through the almost solid wall of rain while clinging to the supports of the wooden bridge, I was relieved to see that the mournful groaning was in fact coming from the giant sycamore tree towering over the ruined end of the mill. Over the years I have measured the tree by eye on many occasions, and reassured Donella only recently that it is still at least a yard shorter than the horizontal distance between its base and the roof of the mill cottage.

Now, however, the creaking sycamore looked more than a little taller. Then, as I turned to fight my way back towards the welcoming light above the porch door, I sensed something staring at me through the wall of rain, turned, and came face to face with Helquin the Hunter.

From the top of the wood pile, two greenly glowing eyes reflected the sporadic flashes of lightning, and I reeled back in horror as the thing gave vent to an unearthly screech which cut through the thunder of the storm like a banshee in particularly good voice.

As I stood rooted to the spot, a black shape flew straight at me, over my shoulder and disappeared into the mill porch. Pausing only to summon up my reserves of courage and grab our largest felling axe from the woodshed, I struggled back to the mill to defend my wife from this unknown and awful creature of the night.

Inside, I found Donella sitting in front of the stove, with a large, wet bundle purring contentedly on her lap. Obviously, our feral cat had decided to take shelter from the storm, and immediately fallen under my wife's spell. Over the years, we had often seen a flash of fur and a gleam of teeth as we travelled around the long grass at La Puce, but the owner had never stayed long enough for even my wife to win him over. The arrival of the Great Storm of Néhou had clearly overcome his aversion to human company, and with a sinking feeling I realised we would now have yet another mouth to feed.

I also fear for the future safety of our mouse family, until now comfortably and safely installed in their quarters by the heating tank in the loft.

Approach love and cooking with reckless abandon.

Alleged ancient Tibetan homily

Look after the centimes when you're cooking,
and the francs will grow like onions in horse shit.

Alleged ancient Norman homily

Over the years, we have collected some pretty rum recipes at the Mill of the Flea, and made some even rummer meals. When the nearest shop is more than two miles away and the local restaurant closes for lunch, one learns to be inventive and resourceful when it comes to meal times. My wife regularly raiding the larder for tasty titbits for our wildlife guests also doesn't help with planned catering.

I often receive recipes and accounts of memorable meals and local customs from friends in other parts of France, thus the *mélange* of styles, ingredients and regional peculiarities to be found in the following pages.

The menus in this book have all been road tested by ourselves, and though not meant to represent any general theme or standards save those at La Puce, I hope you will find them as interesting and sometimes challenging as we did.

Menu de Tempête

To start: Hot Goat Salad

This was the first course of a meal cooked after our version of the Great Storm, made on the wood-burning stove with what was available in the larder. As far as I am aware, *Chèvre Chaud* is a common enough dish throughout France, but this recipe is the speciality of one of our favourite restaurants, where any cheeses but the local varieties are permanently off the menu. According to the chef's philosophy, the bacon bits must also derive from Norman pigs who have led a contented life and were personally known to the patron, and the raw egg toppings come only via hens of impeccable ancestry. While not bound by these local conditions, you must also be sure to be liberal with the dressing, and only ice-cold farm cider in earthenware cups should really be taken as a suitable accompaniment.

Ingredients (for four)

A lettuce	Four bacon rashers (streaky is best)
A round of goat's cheese	The dressing (see below)
Four eggs	A stale baguette

Method

For each serving, line the interior of a deep bowl with some lettuce leaves. Cut the bacon into bite-size pieces and fry till *very* crisp. While this is happening, heat up your chip pan ready for the cheese, which you will by now have cut into suitable wedges. Now fish out the bacon and fry small chunks of the stale baguette in the bacon fat till golden-brown and crispy. As you turn the croutons over, dump the wedges of cheese into the chip pan for a few seconds. Rescue them before a melt-down catastrophe occurs, then add the cheese, bacon pieces and the croutons to the bowl.

Add some more bits of lettuce leaf and jumble it all up before drizzling a suitable dressing* over. Crack your egg in half and cleverly tip the contents from one shell to the other till only the yolk remains. I usually throw the white away, but if you wish to show how clever and conservative you are, you can save it to make meringues or seal a leak in your shoe. Balance the half egg shell and yolk on top of the contents of the bowl and serve. Down our way, fastidious eaters tip the yolk over the salad and mix it in. More practical types drink it straight from the shell as a taste bud kick-starter.

* *(For details of a typical Norman salad dressing, see the recipe for camembert croquettes at the end of the next chapter.)*

The main course: Pig Pudding *Flambé*

In any country community, traditional recipes take full advantage of every remotely edible bit of an animal destined for table. The pig is, of course, eminently suited to this credo. In our locality, some traditionalists like to drink the blood of a slaughtered porker while it is still warm. Here is a more civilised (i.e. less squeamish) way of enjoying the full-blooded flavour:

Ingredients (for four)

One large piece of black pudding   Six eating (but sharp) apples
One tablespoon of olive oil   A large lump of butter
A pinch of cinnamon   Some salt and pepper
Two large glasses of calvados or, preferably, home-brew *calva**

Method

Peel and core the apples, then cut into thick slices. Melt the butter in a frying pan and add the apples when the butter is really hot.

26

Turn the slices from time to time until they are a lovely golden brown. Take them out and keep warm in a casserole dish after seasoning with salt, pepper and cinnamon. Cut the black pudding into slices, and brush each side with oil. Fry the slices in the butter, then add them to the casserole with the apples on top. Just before serving, pour one glass of calvados over the pig pudding and set alight. Drink the other glass before you take the dish in to your guests.

*Officially, calvados is the Norman equivalent of posh brandy, but distilled from apples rather than grapes. It is made and sold under licence after being matured in oaken casts for up to a decade, with the finest examples reaching the price of a very good cognac. In the real world of our part of Lower Normandy, the illicit mobile distilling plant arrives at isolated farmhouses in the dead of night, and the going black market rate for a decent bottle of moonshine calva is around a tenner. Some of our more restrained neighbours resist the temptation of seeing off the bulk of their year's supply while (like the pig's blood) it is still warm, and a good vintage will be saved for really important celebrations, like the death of a neighbour who has been trespassing on your land.

Afters: Banker's Quick Dick

In our early days at the Mill of the Flea, our bank manager was a frequent visitor. He claimed he was interested in seeing how the restoration work was going, but I believe he wanted to see how his crazy English customers could spend so much money on such a tiny part of Normandy. He brought his wife to dinner one evening, and she had great fun going nervously through our larder like a missionary in a cannibal's kitchen. Curiously for someone from a nation with, to some other western races, a number of unpalatable ideas of what qualifies as edible, she was fascinated with a packet of shredded suet. When my wife explained it was dried beef fat she dropped the box in horror and fainted clean away. After reviving her with a glass of home-brew *calva*,

Donella knocked up a relatively instant version of spotted dick which the chic Parisienne, to her credit, tried and pronounced almost eatable:

Ingredients (for four)

Six ounces of self-raising flour   Three ounces of shredded suet
Three ounces of sultanas   Lots of golden syrup

Method

Having warned any French dinner guests what they are about to eat, put on a large pan of water to boil. Then gently mix the flour, suet and sultanas together. Even more gently, add water and mix until a good consistency (not too wet) has been formed. Using floury hands, mould into the traditional dick shape, then wrap in foil, making sure to seal the edges. Place in the pot and simmer for around 30 minutes. Only experience will ensure you cook your dick to the turn.

When it is plumply pliable, smother your dick with golden syrup and serve in mouthful-sized portions.

Drinks suggestions

As all I know about wine is that the allegedly better varieties come in bottles rather than boxes or plastic barrels, I am indebted to my friend and vinicultural buff Conrad Barnes for his thoughts on how to best complement some of the courses in these pages. He writes:

As a general guide, you may wish to start your meal with the lighter end of the scale, progressing on to the heavier and stronger wines as you near the finishing post. For the Hot Goat Salad, the strong goat's cheese element suggests a dry-ish but fruity white wine.

You might like to try a Vouvray from the Loire, or a Tokay-Pinot Gris from Alsace, which is probably a little softer than the Vouvray. Given the natural presence of Calvados in the middle course, I find it difficult to come up with a suitable wine to complement the Pig Pudding *flambé*. Perhaps it would be best to clear (or attempt to clear) the palate with a glass of ice-cold cider. The Banker's Quick Dick being a pudding of some substance, a single glass of good champagne might lighten the heart before moving on to liqueurs, coffee and, if dining at La Puce, the inevitable nightcap of *calva*.

Culture Club

If life must not be taken too seriously, then neither must death.

Samuel Butler (English novelist and sometime sheep farmer)

The monthly Annual General Meeting of the Jolly Boys Club took place at the Bar Ghislaine this morning, so we were in full assembly.

There was a new probationary member to welcome, but the main item on the agenda was to decide upon a strategy for claiming compensation after the Great Storm of Néhou. All my friends had dramatic stories to tell about how they had survived the night, and how much they should be able to claim for damage and individual loss and suffering. The fact that none of my co-members are insured for any eventuality in life did nothing to lessen their enthusiasm for receiving full and proper compensation from some official body.

As I arrived, individual speakers were already vying to come up with the most dramatic tale of loss and hurt, and there has already been a motion to ask Paris to declare Néhou a disaster area. One of our members is alleging that his entire herd of cattle was sucked up in a tornado that swept through his field at the height of the storm, and another has been drawing up a claim for losing a roof which we all know was destroyed by a stray shell during the D-Day Allied bombardment.

We also know it is certain that the hard-hearted bureaucrats in Brussels and Paris will ignore our applications and prefer to waste tax payers' money on repairing power lines and roads elsewhere in France, but debating opportunities like these are meat and drink to our club.

Full membership of the JBC is limited to senior members of

the commune, and the numbers tend to fluctuate, depending on who wakes up each morning still breathing. General qualifications also require that the member has lived in or near the village for at least fifty years, and has no less than half a dozen past generations buried in the graveyard opposite the Bar Ghislaine.

Regular attendants at our meetings are Aristide Goulet, a friend and neighbour who lives in a hamlet near La Puce; the giant and fortunately amiable farmer and horse breeder Mr Junot; and Old Pierrot, who claims to have dandled William the Conqueror on his knee in his youth.

Then, of course, there is my special friend René Ribet, our estate manager and mentor in the ways of the countryside, known respectfully in certain local circles as The Fox of Cotentin.

Although I like to think I am fully accepted by this coterie of village veterans and try to play a full part in the life and times in the area, I realise I am and always will be no more than an associate member of their exclusive club. I am, however, allowed to buy the drinks at very regular intervals.

Our meeting place is the bar opposite the church at Néhou, where we are kept in order by the redoubtable Madame Ghislaine. Alone, she has been struggling for years to keep her small grocery shop and bar alive, and in the process provide a focal point for the community.

As in England, village bars and general stores all over France have been closing down with alarming frequency in recent years, and rural communities have lost much more than merely places in which to drink and shop. In our area, even the most remote hamlet-dwellers are making the weekly trip to take advantage of the range and prices at distant supermarkets, and it is obviously becoming more and more of a struggle for Ghislaine and her business to survive. Néhou is now the only village in the area with its own *bar-épicerie*.

Understandably, many people who live in towns seem to find it hard to appreciate the real value of a village bar, and how its function goes far beyond the apparent purpose of supplying a handful of locals with an excuse to sit and drink and talk. Like any English village pub worth its sign, a rural French bar is much more than just a place to buy a glass of beer or wine. It is an unique gathering place for locals to keep their finger on the pulse of local life, and to exchange views of what is happening in the wider world. It is also a place to meet and spread what some unthinking people would dismiss as mere gossip about who is doing what, where, and to whom, and by so doing help keep the community on an even keel.

As any policeman will tell you, local knowledge is the best defence against wrongdoing, and everyone in our area knows that news of unacceptable activity will be in the public domain very soon after it has happened. Within hours of a noteworthy event occurring within a ten mile radius of our village, it will have been reported back to the intelligence gathering centre for dissemination to the men who visit the bar and the women who shop next door. Sometimes, particularly ripe rumours will travel from the bar through the plastic strip curtain into the shop and then on to a hundred homes and families in the course of a single morning. Often, a convenient location for information exchange will be the *pissoir* directly outside the shop window, and which consists of no more than a splash plate made of old enamel posters and a gully which runs along the shop front and into the gutter. A remark made while sharing a companionable shoulder-to-shoulder moment here can be winging its way by moped or lorry to the hinterland of our community before the messenger's toecaps are dry.

Much is made nowadays of the value of the electronic information technology which the pundits claim makes the world what they call a global village. In my opinion, our European leaders would be much better employed in drawing up plans for the subsidy and survival of village pubs, bars and shops than worrying about the optimum curve of a banana or how to get a computer into everyone's front room.

*   *   *   *   *

As our club meeting progressed I found that, as usual, I seemed to be paying for more than my fair share of the refreshments which keep our minds and debating powers oiled and honed.

When I first became an associate member of the JBC, there was no formal system for the buying of club drinks; the general strategy seemed to be to have an empty glass when someone else was buying, and be somewhere else when it was your turn.

Apart from ill-will and unnecessary arguments, this practice meant constant stoppages as members disappeared to stealthily refill their glasses under the pretence of visiting the *pissoir* or going outside to see what the weather was doing or if any sheep had escaped from the van. On return, the whole debate would have to start again, so I proposed an English and therefore seemingly very logical solution. What we needed, I said, was a common pool, with members calling for their glasses to be topped up as the need arose, and the bill shared equally at the end of each session.

Surprisingly, and after an initial stunned silence, my companions agreed to a trial run of the system, but only after a suitable period of oration and debate while I bought another round of drinks.

Following a series of sometimes quite masterly addresses about relative wealth and responsibilities and every Norman's fiercely-held tenets regarding liberty, fraternity and, most of all, equality, a compromise was reached. We would try my idea for a mutual fund, but contributions would be based upon the needs and ability to pay of each member. As a wealthy incomer, this naturally meant that during the experimental period I would have to pay more than the lion's share towards the pot.

Another drawback emerging during the trial run was that each of my fellow members would drink at up to three times his normal speed in order to get his fair share before funds ran out, resulting in some of our number becoming comatose before the day's meeting had got properly under way.

Eventually I gave up trying to organise a formal system, and we now follow a practical routine where the other members have individual tabs for what they consume, while I stand a full round each time I want a drink, which to my colleagues is almost indecently often.

The subject of my rate of consumption is another source for their bemusement with the strange habits of the English, and in past years I have become something of a local attraction. Virtually all my male friends consume more alcohol than me on any given day, but do so over a much greater time span. In the British way, I like to abstain until the day's work is done and then make up for lost time, whereas it is not unusual for my fellow members to start with a glass or two of apple brandy before breakfast, and steadily pace themselves until bedtime.

When I first arrived at the Bar Ghislaine the locals were as amazed at my rate of consumption as the patron was pleased, and after becoming tired of being called from the grocery side of the business to fill up my standard half pint glass every fifteen minutes, Madame Ghislaine sent her husband Bernard on a special mission to Cherbourg. On my next visit, she presented me with a huge litre jug bearing a bicycle bell on the handle. This, she said, should slow me down a little, and when I eventually reached the bottom, I should call for assistance by simply thumbing the bell.

Over the years, the system has worked well, and I know our host has increased her bar takings from visits by drinkers from other villages, some of whom make the trip specially to see Mr Beer Belly's special tankard, or even better, watch in awe as he empties it with breathtaking speed.

*   *   *   *   *

Our meeting moved on through the morning, and as well as enjoying the momentous stories of loss and hardship caused by the storm, I was intrigued to find we have a new probationer. If accepted, he, like me, will be an associate member, and his nomination is all the more surprising in that he has been a resident of our commune for less than a week. On our being introduced, I was also fascinated to learn he has been a corpse for more than twenty years.

At first glance and especially when compared with some of the older members of the Jolly Boys Club, Ronald Dedman seems in remarkably good health for a deceased person. He is a tall man, spare in build almost to the point of being cadaverous, with deep-set dark eyes and a somewhat intense stare, but has a pleasant and even lively manner for someone who breathed his last a couple of decades ago.

According to his story, he has been, as the Norman expression has it, eating dandelions by the roots since the ninth day of October, 1979. During our initial pleasantries, I learned that he recently bought a small cottage overlooking the village cemetery, and already feels quite at home there.

After a large *calva*, I felt emboldened to ask how he came to be dead and yet still above ground, and he put forward his argument with an impeccable French logic that had our fellow members nodding in vigorous agreement.

Whilst alive, he explained, he was an insurance salesman, living quietly in Middlesex with a wife and several children from various previous marriages. One day after the children had grown up and left home, his wife had gone out on a test drive with a used car salesman and never returned. Alone in the house with an aggressive parrot and his collection of exotic fish, he began to think about his life and the uncertainties of what the future held in store. From his recent experiences and as a specialist in life assurance, he knew that the final great mystery of existence is the time and place of our death. Like all other creatures on earth, we do not know when we are to die, but unlike other species, we alone know that we will. He also knew that, though his wife had left him, it was fairly predictable that he would hear from her one day with regard to the division of assets and claims for maintenance for herself and even the car which had been the vehicle of her departure.

Being an organised and hopefully logical person, it seemed clear to him that he could remove most of the uncertainty of what lay ahead by simply ceasing to be. Deciding to make the date of his next birthday also the date of his demise, he sold the house and everything in it (including and especially the parrot and fish), liquidised all his other assets, then set about the business of becoming a non-person.

Using his special skills and knowledge, he posted a notice of his passing in the local newspapers, informed all the proper authorities, then boarded the night ferry from Dover to Calais with nothing more than a large suitcase. With his new and deliberately ironic name, he has been living peacefully in France ever since, moving on when it suited him and his circumstances. Now, he feels it is time to settle down, and is sure that in the village of Néhou, he has found a spiritual home for the rest of his death.

Having heard our probationary member's story and noted his apparent sincerity, it seems to me that there is more to Mr Dedman's philosophy than simply employing a ruse to escape from the system.

From the way he listed and detailed the advantages of being deceased, our new resident actually *believes* he is no longer alive. Predictably, the idea of escaping from all the tiresome responsibilities of life held great appeal to my fellow JBC members, though there was a notable exception.

As our resident immortal, Old Pierrot obviously felt that his thunder was in danger of being stolen by someone who, while not claiming to have lived for ever, has apparently beaten the Grim Reaper at his own game.

*   *   *   *   *

The final item on the agenda for today's meeting was the shock news that the English are claiming the Bayeux Tapestry as their rightful property.

According to a body of Oxford academics, the cloth was designed and made in Canterbury, and should be returned forthwith. With the assurance from Old Pierrot that he personally witnessed the artefact being created in the Cotentin, with the team of seamstresses led by a neighbour and friend of his, a motion was passed to write to Paris and demand that as well as refusing to surrender, the appropriate authority should actually return it to its rightful home for permanent display in the Néhou village hall.

An additional item of more agreeable news from overseas was that a Frenchman has been appointed to solve the problems of the Millennium Dome. There was divided opinion on how the alleged former car park supervisor at Paris Disneyland will fare, but general agreement that the food will be good, and that if the new boss has any sense, he will close the place at weekends and on public holidays.

The JBC Drinker's Diet

The following recipes were kindly donated by various members of the Jolly Boys Club. Being French and particularly Norman, they are to a man convinced they were born with an intimacy, knowledge, understanding and talent for cooking denied to other races. To my certain knowledge, some of our members exist solely on the calories and nutrients derived from a liquid diet, yet all of them seem to know about food, and how to prepare, cook and serve it, and take great delight in proving their skills at least verbally. I once sat through a three hour debate on the best way to skin a rabbit, and it is the only time I have seen my friends come really close to exchanging blows.

To start: *Soupe à l'ivrogne* (drunkard's soup)

This is a particular favourite with all JBC members. As with so many popular national dishes, this traditional recipe has at some time been adapted to suit local preferences and available ingredients. Elsewhere in France, white wine would be the chosen alcoholic constituent. In some abstemious households, the wine would even be replaced by stock or water to make a teetotal version. Needless to say, as far as our club members are concerned, all other ingredients excepting the cider may be dropped, and often are.

Ingredients (for four)

Some olive oil   450 g chopped onions
8 slices of baguette   225 g suitable (meltable) cheese
300 ml stock   600 ml (a good pint) of dry cider
Some salt and pepper

Method

Heat the oil in a frying pan, then brown the onions. Put layers of the bread and cheese into an earthenware casserole, finishing with a generous layer of cheese. Spread the onions on top and pour over the stock and the cider, and season. Put the pot into the oven for around twenty minutes or until the cheese has melted.

Main course: Chitterlings *à la* Néhou with Camembert Croquettes

Not to put too fine a point on it, chitterlings are the cooked intestines of a pig or other suitable animal. If cooked wrongly, they taste (one imagines) like burned cycle tyre innertubes. If treated properly, they are surprisingly good. I once had dinner with a fastidious type who blanched at the idea of trying this dish of the day at a posh Bricquebec restaurant. To be safe, he plumped for the sausages, and pronounced them not only more civilised and typically English, but delicious. I didn't like to tell him that his *andouillette* bangers were, in fact, made of exactly the same bits of another pig.

Ingredients (for the chitterlings)

Some cleaned chitterlings
2 tablespoons of strong mustard
4 dessert spoons of *crème fraiche*
Some calvados (hopefully home-made)

Some apples
2 sprigs of fresh tarragon
Salt

Method

Score the chitterlings so that the skins do not burst during cooking. Wrap them separately in cooking foil and grill for around a quarter of an hour, turning once during cooking. While they cook, take the stems away from the tarragon and chop finely. Blend the cream and mustard, then heat gently in a heavy-bottomed pan. Add salt to taste. Lay out the chitterlings and serve with the sauce, the camembert croquettes and a big dish of finely-chopped pieces of apple. Drink the calvados.

Ingredients (for the croquettes)

1 camembert	Some butter
2 eggs	A large onion
2 tablespoons of *crème fraiche*	Cayenne pepper
Some flour	Some nutmeg
Some breadcrumbs	Some dry cider
Some lemon juice	

Method

Preparing the sauce Normande:

Finely chop and fry the onion in some butter until it is golden. Add 30g of flour and the same amount of butter and work together to make a roux. When it is thickened, add 250ml of the cider. Beat the mixture and season with salt, pepper and nutmeg. Take off the heat and mix in 250ml of cream, and a dash of lemon juice.

To make the croquettes, crush the camembert and mix in three tablespoons of the *sauce Normande* to help soften it. Then mix in some of the *crème fraiche*. Having beaten the eggs in a bowl, shape the croquette mixture, dip in the egg, and roll first in the flour and then in the breadcrumbs. Fry your croquettes in hot oil till golden brown, then drain and serve with the chitterlings.

NB. You may also wish to add a Normandy-style lettuce salad to this interesting meal. Basically, the salads round our way consist of no more than a few lettuce leaves bathed in a vinaigrette made from *crème fraiche* and, of course, some cider vinegar. A more detailed recipe for Normandy Lettuce may be found on page 134 of *René & Me*, a highly recommended book by the same author.

Afters: *Poire flambé à la Vieux Pierrot*

This simple but delicious dish is a long-standing Norman speciality, but its invention is claimed by the oldest member of the Jolly Boys Club. In strict translation, *flambé* simply means 'to set light to', and Old Pierrot says that he created the original recipe early in the 18th century, when a siege he led on the former *château-fort* at St Jacques resulted in a fire in the cellar, which, along with many barrels of calvados, was full to bursting with the year's pear harvest.

Ingredients (for six)

6 pears	2 egg whites
50g sliced almonds	30g butter
80g caster sugar	50cl calvados
80g icing sugar	A pinch of salt

Method

Peel the pears, core and de-pip, then cut into slices and dust with the caster sugar. Heat the butter in a pan and gently cook the fruit for five minutes or so. Pour on the calvados and set alight, then lay the fruit out in an ovenproof dish. Now sieve the icing sugar into a basin and add the salt and egg whites. Place the basin over a saucepan of simmering water and whip the egg whites until stiff and shiny. Spoon over the pears, dot the dish with sliced almonds and then brown under the grill for a few minutes.

Drinks ideas

As George's colleagues in the JBC seem to have the alcoholic content of the whole meal more than covered, I will merely attempt to come up with a suitable accompaniment for the *entrée* and afters. For the chitterlings and sauce, I would try the dry, lightness of a young-ish southern Minervois. For the boozy pears, why not splash out on a really good sweet Sauternes/Barsac?

Home cooking

Good fences make good neighbours.

Robert Lee Frost (American poet)

W e are off to visit a neighbour, but not before I have stuck a plaster over a nasty gash on my forearm.

The culprit is Cato the feral cat, who has now become, according to my wife, fully domesticated. Since taking shelter with us in the mill cottage, he has obviously decided that the guarantee of three square meals a day and all found is much more of an attraction than pursuing his former and proper routine of living off the land and following the general job description of a wildcat.

He now spends his days basking in my armchair in front of the woodburning stove, stirring himself only at mealtimes and to attack me when I come on to the premises. If it can be said about a cat, the creature is obviously barking mad.

Cato is clearly devoted to Donella, and I think he has decided that the best way he can ingratiate himself with her is to attack me. I have named him not after the Roman orator, but for Peter Sellers' oriental manservant in the *Pink Panther* movies, as he has lately taken to secreting himself around the cottage as I approach, then leaping upon me as I come through the door.

My wife says that all cats like to play mock-fighting games, but I think Cato sees me as competition and will not be happy until I have either been frightened off or despatched permanently.

As I dress my wound, I make a mental note to have a quiet word with the hunting club at the *Café de Paris* in Bricquebec. I shall draw vivid word pictures of the Beast of La Puce, and tell them that he is decimating the local small bird and mammal population that is their rightful quarry. They are mostly rotten shots, but even they should be able to draw a bead on a lethargic tom-cat.

Seeing how well he has settled in, I think the main problem will lie in persuading Cato to leave the comfort of my armchair and venture outside when the shootists are to hand.

*   *   *   *   *

It has been an interesting evening with my fellow Jolly Boys Club member Aristide Goulet. We have been friends for almost a decade, but today was the first time we had been invited to visit his home. By local standards this is good going, as an official invitation is a signal honour, and shows we have been accepted at least by him as fully-fledged members of the commune.

Aristide lives not far from La Puce in the tiny hamlet of Le Mignon, and leaving the metalled road and taking to the mostly unbeaten tracks of the interior is like entering another world and time. In France, there are no cities, and even Paris is technically a town. Villages may vary in official and actual population from a few hundred to several thousand depending on how the commune cares to declare and define itself, but a hamlet is always a hamlet.

Rarely comprising more than a handful of houses, a Norman *hameau* is about as rural and isolated as you can get without living completely on your own in the middle of nowhere. I assume there must be an occasional census of all these tiny patches of humanity, but I am sure many of them must escape official registration and attention, and exploring the miles of lanes and dirt tracks in our vicinity, I often stumble across a new collection of homesteads where families have gone about the day-to-day business of living for hundreds of years in contented isolation.

Rather than enjoying contact with other people, being cut off from the rest of civilisation has naturally inclined some hamlet-dwellers to a liking for their own company, and even a mistrust of anyone from the outside world. It is alleged locally that the residents of some hamlets in our neck of the woods make a practice of digging potholes in the lanes leading to their community to

47

dissuade foreigners from nearby villages visiting or even passing directly by their front doors.

This is probably an exaggeration, but people in many of the groups of cottages dotted around in our area certainly seem to prefer to be left alone to get on with their lives. This attitude has inevitably led to rumour-mongering in some towns about all sorts of illicit or immoral goings-on in these closed communities.

I have never heard anyone in our village accuse the residents of a local hamlet of indulging in devil-worship or the odd spot of cannibalism, except, of course, in the case of those homesteads surrounding our rival village of St Jacques de Néhou.

*　　*　　*　　*　　*

As Victor the Volvo bounced up the winding track towards Aristide's home, I waved at a grubby toddler playing in the front yard of a tumbledown cottage. She stared at me for a moment, then turned and scampered inside, doubtless to tell the rest of the family about the invasion.

On the opposite side of the track, a woman who could have been any age from sixty to a hundred was absent-mindedly beating a donkey attached to a small cart on which rested a single milk churn. When she saw me, the woman pointed a claw-like hand in our general direction and mouthed what could have been a greeting or a curse, then watched as we bumped by her front door.

Apparently disappointed when Victor did not explode in a ball of fire, she shrugged, then returned her attention to administering corrective treatment to the donkey.

As Donella negotiated our way past a tank trap obviously left over from the D-Day battles and now serving as further discouragement to unwanted visitors, I sat back to muse on the life of real country people in the Cotentin. Our commune is little more than twenty miles from the bustling and sophisticated port of Cherbourg, yet many people here lead a life which would probably be as unimaginable to the average French town dweller as to the millions of British visitors who arrive at the ferryport each year. Apart from the day-trippers mounting booze and cigarette raids on the nearest hypermarket, most British holidaymakers arriving in the Cotentin drive straight out of town and race off down south, obviously intent on escaping from our area and reaching Real France with the minimum delay.

As far as I can make out, the mythical place they are heading for starts somewhere north of the Loire valley, and is a land of ubiquitous wine and sunshine where characterful characters in berets and striped sweaters live a simple but richly fulfilling and contented life.

In my opinion and experience, Real France doesn't get any more real than in the Cotentin. To visit an ancient hamlet which has not been taken over and gentrified by wealthy commuters is to see what life in the countryside in England must really have been like less than a hundred years ago. Contrary to what the designers of chocolate box covers would have us believe, it could not have been either pretty or easy.

Nowadays, times are less brutal, and old and unemployed people in our area can have a fairly comfortable life away from the conveniences of urban life. But it can be a long walk to the picturesque well on a freezing morning, and given the choice, many would probably opt for a centrally heated apartment and pavements beneath their feet. To my wife and I, the occasional discomforts of living in the countryside are as nothing when compared to the rewards, but we are in an immensely privileged position, and only really play at being children of the fields.

I was once taken to task by a visiting travel writer who accused me of insulting Norman country people by my descriptions of their 'squalid' lives in tumbledown cottages, sometimes with no proper kitchens, bathrooms or even running water. After a few *calvas* in the Bar Ghislaine, I took him on a tour of some of the more remote dwellings in our area, and showed him how many people have to live. I read his article in a posh Sunday supplement a few weeks later, and didn't see a word about our trip or the people he met.

It seems to me that many middle-class British people who call themselves francophiles like to think of all rural French people as being reassuringly happy with their lot, having simple values, low expectations and quaint and endearing habits. In my experience, there are as many different types of people in the countryside where I live as there are in the towns. For me, the main distinction lies in the way rural people seem to have a greater understanding of the realities of nature and country living and relative values. The 15th-century philosopher Michel de Montaigne said he could look out of the window of his château and see many better, happier and wiser people than he had met at university.

This is exactly the sort of thing that privileged people say and at least pretend to think about relatively poor country dwellers, but I have never heard them say it about people who work in factories, or indeed, about their own cleaners and nannies.

One thing is for sure as far as my views on rural life and its rewards and drawbacks are concerned: I can think of many worse ways to spend the day than being in the heart of the French countryside on a crisp spring day with the land coming alive to the prospect of summer, and my wife and I on the way to visit a friend who is reputed to have the finest collection of vintage home-brew apple brandy in the region.

*   *   *   *   *

As we ventured further along the track, a curl of smoke above the *bocage* showed we were nearing our friend's cottage, and that he was at home. No self-respecting Norman would burn good wood and waste precious heat on an empty house.

The last time we drove by, Aristide's aged mother was vigorously weeding the garden, wearing a voluminous and dense black floor dress and severe bonnet despite the heat of the day. After the funeral of the mayor of Néhou four years ago, she wore the same outfit, and insisted on walking the three miles home though we and other villagers offered her a lift. Aristide said she had never been in a car in her life, and thought they bred idleness and unhealthy thoughts about what may lie over the next hill. Madame Goulet died just before her hundredth birthday last year, and now, as far as we know, our friend lives alone.

Alerted by the sound of Victor's springs groaning as he lurched to a stop beside the broken gate, Aristide appeared from an outbuilding and gave us a cheery wave. He was wearing his favourite green overalls and gumboots, and carrying a large and very rusty bucket.

According to the senior members of the Jolly Boys Club, Aristide Goulet is a mere youngster at seventy, but he looks at least ten years younger. Very unusually in an area where the pastime is the norm rather than the exception, Aristide is a non-smoker, and is therefore regarded as something of a health fanatic by his colleagues in the JBC.

He does, however, more than make up for his abstinence from tobacco with his daily consumption of alcohol. Like most of the customers at Ghislaine's bar, he would never dream of wasting money on bottled beer or spirits over the counter, but is reputed to have one of the finest cellars of mature home-brew *calva* in the region. As a small gift, I have brought him a case of beer and a bottle of malt scotch, which, in the opinion of most local people I know, is the only drink from outside France worth having in the house.

Without too many worries about impeding the flow of passing traffic, we left Victor blocking the track and followed Aristide as he returned to the outhouse alongside his cottage. He pumped my hand, then gave Donella the four kisses reserved for close friends in Normandy as I tried to massage the life back in to my fingers.

Like many of the men in our neighbourhood who work on the land, Aristide is short and wiry rather than broad, but tremendously strong. The trick seems to be the way they use their bodies, with minimum effort giving maximum return. I have seen Aristide casually handle a bag of animal feed which I would have had trouble lifting from the ground, and when I tried to teach him arm-wrestling after a long session in the Bar Ghislaine, he toyed with me out of sheer politeness for several minutes before pushing my hand down as if I were a child.

Apart from his build, ruddy face and perennial workwear, Aristide is not a stereotypical Norman countryman in appearance. He does not favour a monumental moustache, his hair is always immaculately cut and dressed, and his features fine. In a suit and tie, he would look more like a company executive than a rural bachelor, and he is as scrupulous in his manners as in his grooming. Our friend is one of nature's gentlemen in the true and unpatronising sense of the expression, and I have greatly valued his advice and friendship over the years.

Having arrived in the outhouse, I saw that the smoke curling above the red-tiled rooftops of his property came not from his home, but from the open fire blazing in the middle of the dirt floor. A metal tripod sat above the dancing flames, and from it hung a smoke-blackened cauldron. Obviously, Aristide had been in the throes of some home cooking, and prefers the traditional method of making his evening meal.

Inspecting his work, I pantomimed an appreciative sniff, and when I asked what he was preparing, he modestly said something dismissive about chicken. I would also have liked to ask him for his personal recipe for the odoriferous *pot-au-feu*, but feared my patois would not be up to it. Like most of our friends in the area, Aristide chooses to speak his own version of the *lingua franca*, and even after all our years as honorary members of the commune, I still find difficulty in the fine tuning when individual nuances and useage come into play.

Becoming aware that we had lost Donella, I heard a deep braying from the field behind the outhouse, and realised my wife had zeroed in on the nearest animal. Leaving the stew to its own concerns, we went to join her, and I found myself looking down the bent barrel of a Sherman tank.

The back of Aristide's tiny Renault is always low on the springs due to the amount of scrap metal in the back, and I knew that he made a weekly trip to the town of Valognes to trade in sorted amounts of copper and brass, but until my visit had not realised the scale of his operation.

The field behind his cottage was completely filled with hundreds of cookers, washing machines, car parts, mangles and other redundant domestic appliances. But dominating the domestic scrapyard and looming out of the twilight like an advancing army frozen in time stood a collection of war machines that the original owners obviously did not think worth salvaging. Immediately in front of us were the remains of an American army ambulance, with windows and roof gone and the back filled with old radiators, boiler parts and window frames rather than patients. Alongside were the remnants of a German staff car, with an ugly blast hole where the unfortunate officer might well have been sitting at the time of impact. Near by stood a brace of battered khaki motorcycles, one with what looked like a nasty bloodstain on the petrol tank.

Though not an expert in these matters, it seemed to me that the otherwise unremarkable scrap yard held a collection of WW II vehicles which would be worth much more to a collector than the value of our friend's home and all the land surrounding it.

*   *   *   *   *

Later in the evening, and we were to be found gathered round a huge dining table in the kitchen, with drinks in hand and the past in mind.

The leaping fire threw long shadows across the room, animating the severe Norman faces looking out from rows of sepia photographs on the walls, and Aristide had been telling us about his life and times growing up on the farm where five generations of his family have lived and where one day he will die. It might not be a grand *manoir*, he said, but it is his home and full of memories. He had told us of his boyhood in the hamlet, and how his family and their neighbours were hosts to the occupying German forces before the D-Day landings. From this period of his young life, he said, he had learned that men were not always to be judged by the uniform they wore, and that war and killing is as pointless as it has been inevitable throughout the ages.

The evening flew by as we learned more about our friend in a few hours than over the past decade, and the fine *calva* that eased our conversation caused me to forget my manners as a guest in a rural household. Bedtime comes early in our area, and polite visitors know the rules for leaving well before they outstay their welcome.

Despite my wife's increasingly obvious signals, I made no move to leave the comfort of our friend's fireside, and had earlier broken another prime directive of the country visitor's code. Aristide had taken us on a tour of his farmyard, and I had dutifully admired his henhouse. When I asked if the inmates were good layers, he presented me with a dozen still-warm eggs. As soon as I complimented him on the quality of his *calva*, he gave me a lemonade bottle full. Too late, I realised I had been ignoring the ritual where an enquiry or a compliment is also an obligation to the host. Feeling hungry and immune to my wife's kick beneath the kitchen table, I then decided to deliberately use the custom to further advantage, and said I hoped we were not keeping him from his dinner, and that the food in his cauldron would now surely be in peak condition.

Apparently forgetting his own manners, Aristide looked quizzically at me and shrugged, said something about me not liking what was in the pot, and made no move to get up from the table. He appeared even more bemused when I dropped all subterfuge and said I would like to try some anyway, then went to fetch a steaming plateful of the stew.

He was quite right, and it was not to my liking, but out of politeness, I followed the ritual and complimented him effusively on his skills and asked for more. Still refusing to join me, he sat and watched with the look of a man trying to understand a tax form as I smacked my lips and cleared another heaped plate before finally acknowledging Donella's attacks on my shins, and getting up to leave.

Back in the car, I began to feel a little queasy as Donella backed Victor away from the gate. By the light of the fire from the outhouse I saw Aristide walking back in to the outhouse, and remarked that there was at least one Frenchman in the world who is not much of a cook.

As our friend reappeared with a steaming bucket and made for the hen coop, my wife said rather tartly that even she knew enough patois to grasp what Aristide had said about the contents of the bubbling cauldron. Rather than saying that the stew had been made of chicken, he had been telling me that it was *for* the chickens.

With a triumphant sniff, she said that she hoped the poor birds would not go short on their supper because of my stupidity, and winding down the window on my side, warned me grimly not to be sick over Victor's paintwork.

*   *   *   *   *

Next morning, and after a restless night I am woken by the sound of an angry hornet approaching the mill cottage. Our visitor will be Patrick the Post, making his usual early start to escape from his marital bed and its unrelenting duties. In our part of the Cotentin there appears to be a limited selection of Christian names, and because of intermarriage, it is also not uncommon for people to share the same family as well as first name.

As in small Welsh rural communities, the tradition is to identify an individual by adding a job title or, if they are not usually employed, a suitable adjectival description. Apart from our local postman, we have a Patrice the Autobus, Patrice the Tractor, and Young, Small, Big, Very Big and Completely Mad Patricks. There is also a legendary character known in Jolly Boys Club circles as Patrice the Donkey, but having shared a visit to the *pissoir* with him, I believe his nickname has more to do with what he keeps

55

in his trousers than in his stable.

Leaning out of the bedroom window, I give our postman a fairly cheery good-day and throw him the key to the porch door. Normally, I would not dream of locking our cottage at night, but Cato had been out for a rare nocturnal prowl and I did not want him coming home and catching me asleep and defenceless.

With a mournful salute, Patrice dismounts from the garish yellow moped which comes with the uniform, official goggles and rent-free cottage in St Jacques. He is short, even for a Norman, and bears a permanent look of woe which is not helped by the hugely luxuriant moustache which emphasises his almost non-existent chin. Emerging from beneath the fronds of the nicotine-stained bush, a hand-rolled cigarette is permanently welded to his somehow inappropriately sensual lower lip. As he smokes even while riding his *mobylette*, it is said that he gets through at least a quarter of a kilo of monstrous home-cured shag tobacco a day.

Inside, our pessimistic postman dumps a satisfyingly large pile of mail on the table, and waits for me to persuade him to stay for a coffee and *calva*. The ritual protestations over, he pours the home-made brandy directly into his coffee cup, pats his moustache to check that he has not left a cigarette installed, drinks deeply and then tells us all the latest news from around the area. As we know, he will call on a score or more customers every day, and take a drink with at least half of them. It is, he says, impolite to refuse hospitality, and he also feels it his duty to provide jolly company for the lonely people on his round.

While he concentrates on rolling his twentieth cigarette of the day, I make the mistake of asking how his health is, and he tells me in great detail. Patrick is a man who will always find a cloud in a silver lining, and like so many of his countrymen, is a complete hypochondriac. Today, the main subject for his concern is the size, texture, consistency and even colour of his first bowel movement of the day, and I ask Donella to put our morning porridge on hold till he has finished the tour of his inner workings.

Eventually duty calls, and after refusing a third *café calva* he wishes us better health, wealth and happiness than he could ever hope for, and departs to cheer up his next client, leaving us to divvy up and eagerly explore the pile of envelopes on the kitchen table.

As a general rule and providing I get to the post first, Donella opens all the uninteresting and threatening-looking envelopes, which are usually those with windows in them. It is my job to open and read the ones with a hand-written address, especially those which look like they might contain what my wife sarcastically calls my fanmail, or even a cheque from a reader ordering a book direct from the author.

This morning, I am delighted to find we have a letter and recipe from distant neighbours. Tony and Doreen Simpson live in the Suisse Normande, a particularly hilly and heavily wooded area just inside the Orne department, and a place which more than lives up to the undulating splendours suggested by its name.

They are veteran settlers, and have had even more experience of the vagaries of buying property in France than us, in spite of (or perhaps even because of) Tony's past calling as a solicitor. Thanks to the inheritance laws, the previous owner of their house had to contend with no fewer than twenty seven individuals with a part-claim to the property. And when the Frenchman had finally restored their new home, his wife had refused to move in after a dispute with her mother-in-law, who lived almost exactly opposite.

The French couple's loss was the Simpson's gain, and our friends now spend their days living a full and interesting life which includes experimenting with regional recipes and enjoying the goings-on across the road when the neighbours meet *en famille*.

The Simpson's Normandy Select

To start: *Coquilles Saint-Jacques au cidre*

The scallop is, of course, the symbol of St Jacques (curiously, the French have no nearer equivalent to St James), and the shells were used to mark the ancient *Santiago de Compostela* pilgrim route through France to Spain. Fittingly for this recipe, the old trail through the Cotentin peninsula went right by the farmhouse door at La Puce. This delightfully Norman-ised version sensibly employs cider rather than the sometimes bland white wine favoured in other parts of France:

Ingredients (to feed four)

12 scallops
250 ml of dry cider
2 shallots
Salt and pepper and lemon juice

150 grams of *crème fraiche*
50 grams of unsalted butter
1 heaped teaspoon of *fond de poisson* *

Method

Wash the scallops and ensure that any black 'strings' are removed, then finely chop the shallots. Melt the butter in a heavy frying pan. Toss in the shallots and sweat for a couple of minutes whilst stirring with a wooden spatula. Then mix in the cider. Put the scallops, salt and pepper in and cook for no more than five or six minutes for large scallops, less for small. Drain the liquid into a small pan and keep the scallop and shallot mixture warm. Reduce the liquid by half, then mix the *fond* with the *crème fraiche* and add to the reduced liquid. Stir until incorporated and bring gently to simmer. Add the scallops and shallots and serve with a slice of lemon and crusty baguette.

* *Cornflower as a thickening agent and a little fish stock with the cider*

will do just as well if you can't get access to this French equivalent of Bisto.

Main course: *Tourte d'automne*

One of the pleasures of Normandy in the autumn months is gathering in the sweet chestnuts, which grow everywhere (or did until the *grande tempête*). We always gather too many for roasting, and find other ways to enjoy them. This recipe mixes the chestnuts with two essential Norman cooking ingredients: apple and pork. Being a lazy cook, I buy my pastry at the local supermarket. Nowadays, it really is as good as granny used to make!

Ingredients (for four)

250 grams of chestnuts   20 grams of butter
250 grams of finely minced   2 eggs
and very lean pork
250 grams of shortcrust pastry (unsweetened)
250 grams of crisp apples (Cox's are ideal in England.
In France use Boskoop)
100 ml of Rivesalts or a similar strong, sweet wine

(You will also need a 20cm loose-based flan tin)

Method

Pre-heat your oven to 190°C/350°F. Grease the flan tin with half the butter. Nick the chestnuts on one side and place under a medium grill until the skin bursts when they are cooked. Remove the skins and crumble the flesh into small pieces. Peel, core and finely chop the apples. Combine the chestnuts, apples, pork, wine, salt and pepper and one beaten egg. Roll out two-thirds of the pastry to about five millimetres thick and line the flan tin. Prick the base gently with a fork. Spread the filling evenly over the pastry base, and roll out the rest of the pastry to make a lid. Brush the edges of the pastry in the tin with water, place the lid on top and firmly seal the edges. Brush with the remaining beaten egg. Make a small hole in the centre of the crust and insert a vent (a small roll of cardboard about the diameter of a pencil will do). Bake for around 45 minutes until golden brown, then let it rest for ten minutes. Remove the vent, melt the remaining butter and brush over the surface. Serve your *tourte d'automne* with a crisp salad. In the unlikely event that any is left over, it is just as nice eaten cold the following day.

Afters: *La Teurgoule*

The origins of this Norman speciality are somewhat obscure. One theory is that it originated in Honfleur in the 18th century, with the recipe brought back from foreign ports by seafarers. Another claim is that the idea for this filling rice dish has its origins in Caen, invented by necessity after a particularly poor corn harvest in the 18th century. Whatever its history, *La Teurgoule* is sold throughout Normandy in *charcuteries* and *boulangeries*, where the baker makes canny use of the residual heat in his ovens by cooking the dish for more than 8 hours at a very low heat. Such is the popularity and pride in *La Teurgoule*, that there is an annual competition for amateur and professional cooks, staged by the grandly-titled *Confrérie des Gastronomes de la Teurgoule de Normandie*. Not bad for a humble rice pudding!

Ingredients

2 litres of full cream milk   150 grams of pudding rice
200 grams of caster sugar   A pinch of salt
2 level coffee spoons of powdered cinnamon

Method

Mix all the dry ingredients together in a round, deep bowl, preferably earthenware, and certainly not metal. Slowly pour in the milk so that the rice grains remain at the bottom of the bowl. Place the bowl in a very hot oven (230°C) for about an hour, then reduce the heat to the lowest possible setting and leave to cook for eight hours or so. (If you are using an electric oven, put a bowl of water in with the *teurgoule* to provide some moisture.)

Whilst the *teurgoule* is at the high heat, a crust will form on the top, and this should be left undisturbed until cooking is complete. Connoisseurs eat the dish with the crust intact, while fussy eaters will remove it before serving! Serving suggestions include cream, jam or, naturally, a dash of calvados.

Drinks proposals

Although scallops are less salty than oysters, fruity flavoured wines are negated somewhat by any strong seafood tang. Perhaps a good Muscadet de Sèvre et Maine or a dry, crisp Chablis would work best with the *Cocquilles Saint-Jacques*. Since white roast meats like pork have no really pronounced flavour, they benefit from being accompanied by delicate red wines. Perhaps a Beaujolais-Villages (Duboeuf) or even a Côtes-du-Rhône would suit the tart. The classic rice pudding suggests a good white Burgundy, a Meursault or a white Rhône like a Hermitage. If you have a really sweet tooth, something along the lines of a Muscat de Beaumes de Venise might be your selection.

Field Day

God made the countryside, and man made the town.

William Cowper (English poet)

I think I may be turning into a werewolf.

Early this morning, my wife found me standing naked in front of the landing mirror, nervously measuring the increase in hair growth from various orifices. After persuading me to dress, she gently led me to the kitchen table and invited me to share my fears.

Over coffee, I explained how I have suspected for some time that Cato is more than just a domesticated feral cat, and now have the evidence.

To begin with, he is far bigger than any cat I have seen, and infinitely more ferocious. His fur is more wolf-grey than the usual variety of cat colour, and his atttacks on me show he prefers fresh, warm blood to a saucer of milk. Also, although he strikes at any given opportunity, I have noticed that the assaults become more frenzied as the moon reaches its full bloom each month.

Finally, the terrible truth is that I have become increasingly aware of excess hair growing from my ears and nose and even down my back. Cato has drawn my blood on regular occasions, and it seems inarguable that he has infected me with the ancient curse of lycanthropy.

All these physical manifestations indicate that I am doomed to become a hybrid creature, and my fate will be to wander the night and howl at the moon as the transformation from man to beast becomes complete.

After listening to my submission, Donella refuses to concede that she is married to a changeling.

Cato, she says, is just an ordinary cat who has been living off his wits since our neighbour and his original owner died two years ago. The poor creature has been the quarry of every passing hunter with a gun, and it is not surprising that he has formed a dislike for men. As he connects the male species with danger, it is also little wonder he has taken against me. Cats are also particularly sensitive to emotions, and Cato can obviously detect my dislike and fear. All I have to do is show him a little affection, and all will be well between us.

As to the so-called evidence of my transmogrification, I may not have noticed that all men grow hair as they become old. It is one of nature's prime ironies that as the weaker sex loses its vigour and virility, hair disappears from the head but grows even more freely elsewhere. A more balanced look in the mirror will show me that it is age and not the curse of the werecat which is causing the sprouting from my nose and ears and threatening to turn my eyebrows into a pelmet. It is also quite natural for bearded men to have hair on their faces.

If I were truly suffering from lycanthropy, my hearing would be improving not getting worse, my eyesight would be keener and not fading, and my teeth would be stronger rather than becoming looser. In short, it is the passing years which are responsible for the metamorphosis. Perhaps I should realise that I am no longer young and, like her, accept the ageing process more gracefully.

I sit around and think about this for a while, but am not convinced. Just yesterday, I tell her, I went in to the butcher's shop at Bricquebec and found myself strangely disturbed by a plate of freshly-set blood pudding on the counter.

My wife continues to scoff at my fears, and recommends we spend the day out and about on our land to work off my unhealthy mood. We have been cooped up in the mill cottage for most of the winter months, and it is time to celebrate the arrival of new life and promise for the year ahead.

Besides, she adds, if I get lucky I might just stumble upon the last surviving rabbit in the Cotentin, and so be in a position to test my allegedly wolfish lust for really fresh food and warm blood.

*   *   *   *   *

We start our field day in the mill garden, and my nose tells me our compost heap is progressing satisfactorily well before it comes into sight.

My wife has become quite obsessed with recycling, and seems quite happy to be growing a huge mountain of decay beside the door leading to our larder. She has also taken to loading the pile with anything which can be said to have organic roots. I now have to carry out a daily inspection of the malodorous heap to rescue unread newspapers and uneaten food, and I'm missing several pairs of my longest-serving and therefore most comfortable cotton underpants.

I also see that the soggy cardboard project is getting completely out of hand. For years, Donella has objected bitterly to the ancient rural custom of myself and male visitors peeing outdoors, but has now found a way of putting the tradition to practical use. Having read about the theory in an alternative gardening book, she has established a pile of old cardboard boxes alongside the compost heap and actively encourages all our friends to pee on it, even watching and directing them where to spray.

As far as I can make out, the theory is that a regular sprinkling with alcohol-rich uric acid will eventually transform the cardboard into a rich and crumbly black fertilizer, but all I can see is a heap of wet and very smelly beer cartons.

Hurrying downwind, we arrive at the grotto where I suggest an early break to enjoy watching the antics of our small and fast-flowing stream as it tumbles down into the stone-walled basin at the start of Hunter's Walk.

Like most ancient mills, La Puce drew its power from a modest water course, and the system for putting the grinding stone into action was as ingenious as it was simple. Behind the mill cottage and alongside the stream which sources at the nearby *manoir du Lude* lies a three-acre field shown on old maps as *le réservoir*. When the miller was preparing for a grinding session, he would lower a stone slab in front of the basin, diverting the stream into the field, which would shortly become a lake. When the grain hoppers were full and all else was ready, he would raise another slab at the working end of the mill and water from the reservoir would crash down on to the wheel, which would duly turn.

The work done and the flour bagged, the miller would raise the slab in the front of the basin, and *le Lude* would resume its eternal journey to the sea. Since the Mill of the Flea fell into disuse at the beginning of the last century, the stone basin has become overgrown with a variety of trees and bushes and makes a delightfully shady and cool retreat from the heat of the summer sun. After a day working on the land, my habit is to strip off and sit on an old tree stump below the curtain of water. My wife says it is not a pretty sight, but I find these philosophical moments very refreshing, and it also helps dissuade the poachers from fishing for the trout that like to gather there.

Above ground and made by man rather than nature, the water basin is obviously not a grotto, but it is a place of magic for me and I have developed a plan to use it to bring in some much-needed revenue. Although our books on life at La Puce have proved surprisingly popular and kept our bank manager at a respectable distance for some years, with no pension or other income we are constantly under pressure to make ends meet. So far, my schemes to make an additional living from the land have not been successful.

Bottling and marketing the water from our well turned out to be a non-starter when analysis showed the contents to be toxic, and other plans for garlic-flavoured car deodorisers, metal detecting weekends to find the miller's legendary crock of gold, a fish-your-own trout farm and even a miniature golf course came to nothing. Local people found the idea of paying good money to walk around a field utterly risible, and it is a long-established custom in our area to fish for free when the owner of the pond is absent. The car deodoriser project was also a flop, as I had failed to appreciate that most French cars smell of garlic anyway. But I am still convinced there is a realistic way we can make some pin money from the land at La Puce.

I know from my correspondence that financial survival in France is also a constant preoccupation with many fellow settlers. The problem usually stems from people falling in love with the idea of living permanently at their holiday home, and moving over with no transferable skills and little if any experience in setting up and running a business anywhere, let alone in a foreign land. The initial and most obvious solution to their problem usually involves using their French home as a money-earner, but it seems to me there are now more British-run *gites* and bed and breakfast businesses in France than there are British holidaymakers.

Some people do find a way to make ends meet, but many proposals seem extremely unrealistic, and we have even received calls and letters from would-be settlers asking if we think there is a market in rural France for such vital services as mobile chiropody, home tarot readings or sex-aid party plans.

Although we have tried and failed with so many projects, I still enjoy the process of considering money-spinning ideas I can adapt to our circumstances, and have recently devised another one which could, this time, be a winner. As we sit on the old railway sleeper bench by the water basin, I explain my latest scheme.

In a recent edition of *Paris Soir*, I read that visitors are now besieging the Grotto at Peche-Merle just to stare in wonder at a series of cave paintings allegedly left there by Cro-Magnon Man. Illustrating the story were photographs of the crude daubs said to represent bison and other animals, and there was even what was claimed to be a 20,000 year-old outline of a handprint, though it looked suspiciously as if it had been sprayed on the walls of the cave with an aerosol paint can. I am sure we could do at least as well, and my plan is to 'discover' a series of ancient frescoes, painted or chiselled into the stone wall behind the curtain of water in our basin. If I can find a friendly archaeologist who will agree they could just possibly have been made by some ancient tribe, we could open the *Grotte de la Puce* to the public, and charge visitors to view the evidence.

Donella is predictably unconvinced that my scheme will work, and anyway abhors the idea of hordes of people invading her treasured acres and frightening her wildlife residents. To win her over, I point out the advantages of having hundreds of people peeing on her cardboard box compost heap every week, and she expresses a little more interest in my latest wheeze as we wander along Hunter's Walk.

*   *   *   *   *

Arriving at the Hobbit Tree, Donella leaves me for a moment so that I can talk to my dear friend Lucky, who now rests forever in the ground below his favourite shady spot.

While she pretends to look for our solitary squirrel, I sit and snivel for a while as I think of what Sir Walter Scott said about dogs. He thought the reason they have such short lives is out of compassion for humans. The longer they are with us, the greater the grief when we lose them. I only had the privilege of knowing Lucky for five years, but I still miss him, and think about him every day. He was only a scruffy, ill-tempered cross-bred collie, but he was my best friend in a way that is inexplicable to people who don't like dogs. My wife and family are more important to me than all the animals in the world, but Donella understands exactly how I feel and leaves me to my thoughts and memories for a long while.

After I have told my darling Lucky all our news and said another tearful goodbye, I blow my nose on a handy dock leaf and we cross the gravestone bridge to the water meadow and the big pond. The makeshift bridge is one of a heap of slabs our friend René Ribet says he was given by the local undertaker after he had spoiled the lettering following a long session at the Bar Ghislaine.

I do not know if this is true, but there are certainly some very oddly spelled names on the slabs, and they have come in useful as a surround to the pond. Even the muskrat finds difficulty in borrowing his escape tunnels through solid marble.

As we cross *le Lude*, I see further evidence that ethnic cleansing has been taking place at the big pond.

When we set it in place, the makeshift stone bridge comfortably spanned the stream, but the banks are clearly getting further apart, thanks to subsidence. They are also riddled with burrows, which means Reggie and Ronnie Cray have been on the move again. I had noticed that membership of the crayfish gang had fallen drastically since the arrival of the muskrat, and assumed he had eaten them. Now I see that large numbers have fled to take up other quarters, and that their new territory already extends to the stone basin.

If they continue to migrate at this rate, I shall have to keep an eye out for news of any sudden collapses of local road bridges, or infants disappearing from the river banks of our nearest town.

At the big pond, we spend a pleasant hour building a cairn of rocks to provide a safe meeting place for the frogs when the mating season starts in earnest, and then as we sit outside the caravan, another Big Idea strikes.

When we first began restoration work at the farmhouse, one of the most physically challenging tasks was to knock holes in the yard-thick walls to provide spaces for extra windows and doors. Afterwards, we were left with hundreds of large stones, and the ruined bread oven and ruined outhouses provided thousands more for repair work and new building projects. Even the bed of *le Lude* is paved with painstakingly dressed stone slabs to help the water to run faster and clearer, and the sandstone and granite rocks seeding the land are seen as nothing more than a hindrance to local farmers.

On a recent trip to England, we visited a garden centre and saw that a modest piece of stone to decorate a pond was priced at almost ten pounds. We, I point out to my wife, have an almost limitless supply of characterful stones, especially if we were to knock down the ruined walls alongside the mill cottage. In England, people are willing to pay ridiculous prices for ornamental stone, while we are surrounded by tumbledown barns and derelict cottages which the owners would sell for a few hundred pounds and then consider the buyer completely mad. All we would have to do is borrow the money to buy up a derelict barn, then hire Patrick The Tractor to knock it down. We could ship the resultant rubble across the Channel and sell it at a huge profit to garden centres or even builders who specialise in making new houses look like old ones so they can put the price up.

Warming to the theme, I say we should actually think seriously about demolishing the farmhouse at La Puce, as the component parts would be worth much more than the value of the building, even in its restored condition.

Predictably, Donella is not keen on the idea, and responds with her own money-making idea which, she says, will not destroy our home in the process. Her frankly unrealistic and even naïve proposal is to create a vineyard on the scrubby slope leading down from the roadside farmhouse to the mill cottage. I open my mouth to list a dozen reasons why her scheme is doomed to failure, then consider her track record for making things grow. Three years ago, she planted a sad-looking twig in the ground after assuring me that it was a red wine vine, and also that it would blossom. I scoffed at the idea, and gave her a geographical dissertation on the wine-growing areas of France, which, apart from Champagne and Alsace, are all well south of Normandy. Although it is well known in the area that my wife can make a walking stick blossom, I was sure her weedy plant was doomed. Now, the single vine is several yards long and produces dozens of bunches of almost edible grapes each autumn.

Based on this success, my wife says she will look at the prospect of a commercial growing project seriously, and will begin by building a network of posts and wires to bear the vines which will produce the first pressing of *Vin Rouge du Puce*. I humour her and pretend to show enthusiasm, but secretly doubt that even she can turn our boggy land into a fruitful and nationally renowned vineyard.

*   *   *   *   *

All is peaceful at the big pond, so we continue our ramble and find we have yet another border dispute at the end of Hunter's Walk.

We are hemmed in on three sides by more than a dozen neighbours, and there is often disagreement with some of them as to exactly where our land ends and theirs begins. This is not because we are foreigners, just neighbours, and it is a drama which is played out daily in our area and, I suspect, in the rest of rural France.

Apart from three friendly farmers and fellow Jolly Boys Club members who own land abutting ours, no fewer than nine people also claim strips of land around La Puce. We have never seen them, but believe some to be people who work in town but who have kept their rural identity by buying up small fields or even parts of them.

In England, one is used to the idea of vast swathes of land belonging to one person. Where we live now, many people own no more than a few square metres, and in extreme cases, would probably kill to protect them. The idea of bridle paths or ramblers' rights are laughable, and to cross from your land on to the terrain of another is to risk certain insult and abuse, and sometimes real injury. Boundaries are marked with lethal rows of barbed wire, and grimly worded placards carry warnings of what will happen to anyone found venturing on to this private part of France. While even Norman countrymen cannot move living trees, the barbed wire fences surrounding La Puce often seem to have a life of their own, and always appear to move in our direction.

This is why we walk our boundaries at least once a week, and in an active period of movement, every day. Sometimes, we arrive in the morning at a boundary and find that the wire and posts have migrated overnight, increasing our neighbour's land by a few precious metres and decreasing ours accordingly. At first I liked to think I was above this sort of petty activity, but over the years I have become infected by the unreasoning rural passion to own a few more yards of unfruitful dirt, or at least prevent a neighbour gaining some of yours. I now spend hours measuring exact distances from immovable landmarks to the existing boundary line, searching for old post hole marks and even leaving strands of cotton stretched from one post to another to detect any covert movements. Donella says the issue has become an obsession with me, but I say I am only protecting our land for future generations of the East family.

I also tell her how unusually privileged and even envied we are to have a stream running through La Puce, and have suggested that she re-read *Jean de Florette* if she needs reminding of the level of emotions disputed land ownership in rural France can arouse.

Today, I see that our northern perimeter has come under attack again. Last week, I spent a whole day erecting rude signs along the exact point where Hunter's Walk ceases to be our property and comes under the ownership of an unknown neighbour.

Careful examination shows that the posts have been carefully removed from their lodgings complete with the concrete I set them in, and replaced at a point more than a metre into our land. If this were not serious enough, the encroachment has put a particularly fine bramble bush beyond our territory, and I am outraged.

My wife attempts to calm me by pointing out that we have more than enough patches of useless bramble to be going on with, but I am determined to stop the incursion. I replant the posts, and decide to call on Aristide Goulet and see if his military scrapyard contains any WW II anti-personnel mines in reasonable working order.

*   *   *   *   *

On our return to the mill cottage we meet Postman Pat parking his moped while keeping a wary eye out for Cato the werecat.

Although he invariably looks like a Norman who has lost a franc and found a centime, Patrice seems in a particularly reflective mood today. His moustache is drooping even more than normally, and he is unusually silent as he hands over our mail and agrees to join me in the porch for coffee and *calva* with hardly a demur.

When I try to avoid the subject of his health by asking him how his wife is, he sighs heavily then says he supposes she is better than nothing. This is bold talk from Patrice, and he does not even glance fearfully over his shoulder as he refers to the formidable Madame Mégere, so I gently press him for details of the latest episode of marital discord.

After taking another gulp of coffee while somehow keeping his cigarette attached to his upper lip, Patrice explains that he has been to the doctor, and has been told he has a serious problem. I wait for the usual graphic description of some trivial ailment, and am deeply shocked when he reveals in almost matter-of-fact tones that cancer of the testes has been diagnosed.

As I struggle to find the right words of consolation and encouragement, he gives a sad shrug and begins to roll another cigarette. For him, he says, it is not the end of the world. The doctor has assured him that a speedy operation will remove the offending items, and with any luck it will spread no further. Frankly, he will not be unhappy to lose his *couilles*, which have caused him so many headaches over the years. He is more worried about his wife's reaction when he tells her about the operation. Madame insists on the fulfilling of his husbandly duties at regular intervals, sometimes more than once a week, and the doctor has told him that marital relations will be out of the question for months to come. Knowing of her preoccupation with matters of the bed, he dreads her reaction. Life will hardly be worth living in the Mégere household for the foreseeable future.

As he completes his sad story, he looks at me in a peculiarly thoughtful way, then asks if I find his wife attractive. On the back foot, I mumble something about her being a fine figure of a woman, and try to recall the French compliment about a woman having plenty of meat on the bone.

Having worked his way steadily through another two *calva* and four cigarettes, Patrice shakes my hand, mounts his official moped and buzzes off up the mill track, but not before inviting me to visit his home next week for evening drinks. He also made a point of suggesting I come alone, and says how pleased his wife will be to see me. I don't know what he is driving at, but I certainly didn't like the way he eyed me up and down as he gingerly climbed aboard his *mobylette*. It reminded me of the way a farmer will look at a bull at Bricquebec market when it is time for his cows to be serviced.

*   *   *   *   *

An hour later, and with Cato safely locked in the woodshed, I am settled in front of a cheery blaze enjoying the latest bulletin from a fellow settler and author who is an eccentric after my own heart.

Christopher Fraser-Wright's family goes back to the time of William the Conqueror and he is of the gentry as well as a true gentleman of heart. He lives with his lovely and understanding wife Ingrid in a 12th-century Templar's castle in the Martel area, and spends his days writing about food, cooking and other glories of life in the area as he struggles to restore the *Maison du Silence* to its former splendour.

At the moment, he tells me, he is engaged in taking the nine-hundred-year-old drawbridge to pieces, and has high hopes that he will be able to reassemble it in full working order. If not, he may be temporarily marooned, and plans to have supplies airlifted above the battlements by the local Montgolfier admiration society.

I relate the story of Lord Chris's latest adventure to my wife, and she says it is some measure of my own state of mental equilibrium that I see nothing unusual in the idea of a man in a castle having his groceries delivered by hot air balloon.

*   *   *   *   *

I am delighted to see that Chris has enclosed a contribution to my collection of regional recipes, and with it news of developments in the yearly battle between two groups of equally passionate hunters.

The first group are the enthusiasts who spend long days on their hands and knees in various woods and spinneys in search of fine examples of the elusive black diamond. Martel is one of the richest areas for truffles, and vast fortunes are said to have been made by those countrymen with a nose for where the best specimens are to be found and how to pinpoint their location. Apart from the assistance of a carefully trained truffle pig, afficianados claim to be able to identify and track down a certain species of insect said to hover above these shyest of fungi. Whole families are to be found crawling around Lord Chris's castle at this time of year, with their rumps in the air, their noses to the ground and their eyes peeled for the legendary truffle-fly.

While any Frenchman would understand and even admire this dedication to the pursuit of the ridiculously overpriced fungal growth, their activities invariably bring the truffle-seekers into direct and often painful confrontation with hunters in search of whatever edible wildlife survives in that part of France. Given the average hunter's enthusiasm for shooting anything that moves, accidents are not unusual, and due to the peculiar posture of the trufflists, buttocks full of buckshot are a common injury. This year, reports my noble friend, there has been the usual tally of peppered arses, law suits and threatened vendettas, and he is working on an invention which, if successful, could avoid further injury and unpleasantness while at the same time providing him with more than enough money to totally restore the *Maison du Silence*.

My aristocratic correspondent is currently engaged in the development of a lightweight pair of chain-mail underpants which would not impede the trufflist's movements, but protect him from the odd salvo when hunting parties come face to arse in the woods of middle France. He got the idea from studying the armour and accessories worn by the original owners of his castle, and has already produced a prototype model.

The only problem now, he concludes, is to find a volunteer to test his iron underpants in the field.

Lord Christopher's Noble Feast

To start: *Omelette Aux Truffes*

Apart from stealing them from a neighbour's land, truffles may be obtained in a number of conditions and containers. If you are not in a position to buy them fresh from the ground at market, they should be readily available in cans and jars from specialist food shops, often slightly pickled in armagnac or some other spirit. If you are lucky enough to get your hands on the fresh variety, you may have to clean them, which is best done with a toothbrush under cold running water. Although it is a practice frowned upon by the *cognoscenti,* truffles are freezable. Some people like to keep them in the larder next to eggs, as the pungent aroma will (I promise you) penetrate the shells and enhance the flavour. Consequently, if you are going to store your black diamonds in a fridge, put them in a sanitised bag unless you like the idea of truffle-flavoured yoghurt.

Ingredients (for four)

6 eggs   1 50g truffle
1 port glass of madeira wine   1 teaspoon of chopped parsley
Salt and pepper
2 tablespoons of duck or goose dripping (I prefer butter)

NB. You will need two frying pans for this recipe (and preferably four pairs of hands).

Method

Shave the truffle into wafer-thin slices and fry in half the dripping or butter. Cook for a minute, though be careful that you do not let the slices get hard. Then add the madeira and the parsley and simmer for another minute. While this is happening, beat the hell out of the eggs, and heat the balance of the butter/dripping in your other frypan. Throw the eggs into the pan and make the omelette with a wooden spatula, or a fork if you must. Garnish with the truffle and serve immediately on a heated plate with a sprinkling of the sauce.

Recommended wine: Try to locate a Château du Cayrou 1988 (from Cahors). I find it helps this luxury omelette slide down a treat.

Main course: *Mique au Petit Salé*
(Dumpling with Salt Pork)

This is a popular local dish though it has international variations, and the dumpling reminds my dear wife of her native Austria. We were served this course by a friend who is a former president of the Terrine Club of Paris. It is a mark of our friendship that she actually agreed to pass on her own recipe, which is not an everyday event amongst chefs in France. Sincere thanks therefore to Madame Claudine Duluat on my behalf, and from all those who will now share the delights of her very special dumplings.

Ingredients
(for six, though for me five, as I get more to eat!)

500g flour	2 tablespoons milk
500g carrots	3 leeks
1 small cabbage	250g softened butter
A pinch of salt	5 eggs
2.5kg salted loin of pork	1 chitterling sausage
20g fresh yeast	

Method

Put the flour in an earthenware bowl, leaving a place in the middle to pour in the yeast, which you will by now have dissolved in slightly warmed milk. Add the salt, butter and eggs, one by one. It is important to knead the mixture well by hand. Continue until the resultant dough becomes supple and elastic. Place the dough in floured cloth and leave to rise for three hours in a warm place. (Under an eiderdown was the traditionally favoured spot.) Meanwhile, rinse the salted pork in cold running water, then dry well to remove excess salt. Put the pork in cold water in a saucepan, then bring to the boil and cook for two hours. Now, peel the carrots, cut the cabbage in two, and wash and tie the leeks in a bunch. Add all this together with the chitterling sausage to the saucepan. Half an hour later, add the doughball and cook for an hour, carefully turning your nascent dumpling over halfway through the process. Serve on a large, warm dish with the dumpling in the centre, surrounded by the meat and vegetables.

NB. Tradition dictates that you divide the dumpling into portions using two forks and never, ever a knife.

Afters: *Charlotte des Templiers*

I find this recipe entirely appropriate, as the original inhabitants of the *Maison du Silence* were Knights Templar. Our region is known for the abundancy and quality of walnuts, reflected in the wonderful selection of breads, cakes and tarts (not forgetting the delicious Denoix *apéritif*) and, of course, walnut oil. A visitor will always know when it is harvesting time, as the bars and cafes will be filled with thirsty workers with black-stained hands.

Ingredients

7cl rum
12 *boudoirs* biscuits
1 tablespoon of walnut liqueur or brandy
200g caster sugar

6 egg whites
300g walnut pieces, finely chopped
250g of softened butter
20cl of sugar syrup
500ml blackcurrant purée

Method

Dissolve 125g of the sugar in one and a half litres of water and cook gently until the syrup is glossy. Add the walnut liqueur and stir quickly. Soak the biscuits in the syrup and line the two long sides of a large rectangular terrine with them. Mix the softened butter, walnuts and rum well. Beat the egg whites until stiff, then pour in the remaining butter, folding in very gently. Incorporate this into the butter and walnut mixture. Put into the terrine and smooth the top, then leave in the refrigerator for at least three hours. When set, fish your Templar's treat out of the terrine and introduce it to the blackcurrant purée, which I am assured can be bought in shops, even in England.

Travels with Victor

Travel makes a wise man better, but a fool worse.

French proverb

A new summer is on the horizon, and this is my favourite time of year.

To be honest, every time of year at La Puce is at some time my favourite time of year, and never more so than when a new season approaches.

In the grip of a seemingly endless winter, I will develop a mild form of cabin fever and long for the first harbingers of spring to free us from seas of mud and the relentless cold. By the end of every summer, I will have grown tired of long lazy days and eternal dusks, and dream of evenings tucked snugly up in the mill cottage with the shutters battened and our early chestnut harvest popping and spitting on the stove.

I like to think that my love of the changing seasons is a sign of my romantic nature, but my wife says it merely shows I am fickle, and the sort of person who always thinks the grass in the other field is greener. In our case it often is, depending on which of our fields you are standing in at the time of making the observation, but it is not worth becoming involved in such a philosophical debate on the subject with a practical woman like Donella.

To be fair, she may have a point about my always wanting to move on to see what is round the next corner, but perhaps my feelings about the approach of a new season also reflect how living in the countryside can bring home the breadth of yearly change and the continuity of nature. Living in town, one only vaguely registers the progress of the year; when it gets colder and darker, it's time to turn on the lights earlier and the heating up higher. You know it has been raining when the pavements are wet. Here at La Puce, the evidence of another year passing by our front door is far more varied and tangible, and we are gloriously exposed to the changes in soul as well as in body.

* * * * *

With the onset of summer, my wife has had another idea for bringing in some much-needed revenue. She has been walking the top fields this morning, and has come up with a scheme that I have to admit sounds entirely practical, and possibly extremely lucrative. She proposes that we stage a household car-boot sale at La Puce. As she says, Normans love going to market, and the nearest place to buy and sell second-hand domestic items is at the distant market town of La Haye-du-Puits.

For some reason, in Cotentin there are none of the used furniture or junk shops which abound in any town in Britain, so local people who need to sell or buy second-hand goods have to visit their nearest *Bonne Affaire* warehouse. These fascinating places are stacked high with everything from a towering hand-carved 19th-century buffet to a period washing machine or nearly-new set of replacement windows that someone for some reason wanted to replace.

As my wife says, nobody appreciates a bargain more than a thrifty Norman, and most Normans we know are very thrifty indeed. There was also a recent article in a national paper which demonstrates the likely appeal of an open-air market at La Puce. The story told how some members of a Chamber of Commerce in Kent staged a car boot sale in Calais to take light-hearted revenge on the yearly French fair at Dover. The organisers thought there might be some mild interest, but were totally unprepared for the thousands of French bargain-hunters who besieged the site and picked it clean.

Inspired by this evidence of the universal attraction of buying something you don't want simply because it's so cheap, my wife is excited about the idea of running our own weekly market. Her plan is to advertise the first-ever boot sale in the area, and charge traders fifty francs to park their cars and display their wares. We will also be able to rent out concessions to sell refreshments, and even invite a selection of the stallholders who work our local market at Bricquebec to take a pitch. If we stage the event on a Saturday, it will not clash with most other markets in the area, and could become an institution. Our top fields are alongside a main road with hundreds of cars passing every day, so we could erect a huge placard and get even more free advertising.

As Donella says, we shall also be able to enjoy the fun of running our own stalls, selling fresh vegetables, home-made preserves, and even all the broken tools and useless bric-a-brac with which I insist on filling her garden sheds. As a final clincher, she challenges me to think of a better place in France to stage a flea market than at the Mill of the Flea. For once, I am in complete accord with one of my wife's schemes, and we spend an enjoyable evening drawing up posters for the great *marché aux puces* at La Puce.

*   *   *   *   *

After almost a decade of living in and exploring the Cotentin, we have been spending some time posing as tourists.

I have been invited to write a personal guide to the peninsula by a ferry company, and the past week has found us standing breathlessly on towering cliffs above the sometimes desolate and always enchanting beauty of the north-western coastline, testing huge bowls of mussels and chips in picture-postcard fishing villages to the east, and revisiting the rolling hills and vales of the heartland. We have been looking at the glories of the Cotentin through a visitor's eyes, and the experience has brought back memories of what first attracted us to the glorious diversity of this magical place.

I have sent outline proposals for the contents of the guide to the ferry company, and they are pleased with my work so far. They have, however, asked me to remove my recommendation for the bed and breakfast facilities at La Puce, and also the full-page advertisement for Madame Ghislaine's bar and grocery store at Néhou.

Today we are on the final leg of our research trip around the peninsula, and will be visiting the ancient town of Cherbourg, then making a pilgrimage down the eastern coast to Utah Beach to try and imagine what it must have been like for the first American troops to storm ashore during the D-Day landings.

As with all travel writers, my pleasure at being able to share my love of the area is tempered with the concern that by promoting the attractions of the Cotentin, I may also be helping to spoil them. My wife says that I should not worry about this, as my books about our life here must have put off as many visitors as the guide may attract.

*   *   *   *   *

There is a saying in the Cotentin that all roads lead to Bricquebec. This is not precisely true, but it is certainly a popular destination for locals and tourists, and is what most guide books (and probably mine) would call a typical bustling and sturdy Norman market town.

Dominated by the remains of a 12th-century castle where any number of historic celebrities are alleged to have spent a night, Bricquebec knows exactly how to make the most of its attractions for the visitor, while never losing its identity as an honest, everyday working town.

Today there is no market, so our favourite local town is relatively quiet. Leaving Victor in the shadow of the castle, we are walking across the square when we narrowly avoid being run down by a battered *deux chevaux* which screams by with horn blaring and a cheery wave from the occupant of the passenger seat.

Dusting myself down, I observe that Ivan the Terrible is teaching a new customer the rules of the road as they are followed in this and most other parts of France. Ivan is a driving instructor of Russian extraction, but is truly French in his attitude to the rights of pedestrians, and spends his working life ensuring that his clients learn to drive in a satisfactorily dangerous manner. He claims that the large number displayed on the dented door of his car shows the tally of successful driving test passes by his former pupils.

Locally, it is alleged that the figure actually represents the number of innocent pedestrians his clients have managed to run down.

With Ivan and his pupil safely around the corner and the distant sound of a collision signalling that they will not be returning for a while, we cross the road to the *Café de Paris* and see through the plate glass window that Freddo the Professor is in place behind the bar, and the local debating society in full session.

There are a dozen amiable bars in Bricquebec, but Freddo's is the most popular with the town's seasoned drinkers and philosophers, and I find the place and patron especially appealing. As with English pubs, every café has its own atmosphere or lack of it, which depends mostly on the type of customers who frequent the premises. They are invariably attracted to the place by the sort of person the proprietor is, so in many ways the whole ambience of any bar or pub will give a fair indication of the character and inclinations of the landlord.

Once upon a time, I fell into the trap of believing that I would make an ideal licensee, and that running my own pub would mean I could drink for free and make a good living from what I do for a hobby. I was to be speedily disabused of this common pub-goer's fantasy, and just one of the problems was that many of my customers seemed completely mad.

My wife said this proved the old adage about like being drawn to like and that our collection of eccentrics, dropouts and committed alcoholics identified with me, but I think that, in this case, the unusual customer profile was merely a coincidence.

We push our way through the comfortable fug, savour the bouquet of good French coffee and rank French tobacco, greet our friends and learn that the subject of the current debate is a foreign visitor who is sitting in the corner and talking to himself. This would not be particularly remarkable behaviour for a local, especially after a long session on market day, but the stranger has confided in Freddo that he is dead.

Walking over to the corner where Ronald Dedman is sitting, I see that rather than communing with an invisible fellow deceased, he is having an animated conversation on a hands-free mobile telephone.

Taking a seat, we wait for our strange new friend to finish his call as I reflect on the peculiar pleasures of being a settler in a foreign land. Although I know we are accepted by this and several other communities in the area, we shall always be intimate outsiders, and this suits us very well. Simply because of the foreign perspective, an everyday visit to a bar or shop can demonstrate aspects of human nature which might pass unnoticed on home ground.

Presumably, there are villages and towns all over Britain with the same sort of people leading roughly the same sort of lives as here, but standing on the outside looking in seems to lend me a singular clarity of vision.

For all sorts of other reasons, being a familiar stranger in what must always be a foreign land is a continuing delight, though I know it is not always so for others in our position. I am often asked what qualities of character best equip a would-be settler for enjoying a life in France, and have spent many hours thinking about and discussing the subject with other Britons who are making a life here. An interest in other people and cultures is of course a prerequisite, but I believe to this must be added a taste for small adventures, a willingness to compromise and a sense of perspective when considering one's place in the greater scheme of things. As any veteran settler will tell you, a sense of humour is invaluable, and, perhaps most importantly of all, an understanding that just because things are done differently in your new homeland, they are neither better nor worse for that; just different.

Another important consideration for all those who wish to make a new life in France is their real reason for wishing to do so. Some people move across the Channel because they genuinely feel at home in France, and some because they think they are escaping from an unhappy situation or life. Often, they are really trying to escape from themselves, which is not possible, even in rural France.

Strangely, the least successful British immigrants seem to be those who claim to be the most ardent admirers of all things French. Invariably, they are the sort of people who appear to think everything about France is as wonderful as everything about their home country is worthless. They are generally snobs, and rarely seem to meet or want to know or understand real French people. Their obvious loathing of every aspect of Britain is usually a mask for deep self-loathing, and I have noticed that many French people find their attitude as strange and sad as we do.

*   *   *   *   *

Ronald Dedman having completed his distant conversation, he takes my hand in a surprisingly lively grip, and becomes extremely animated when I tell him about our visitor's guide to the Cotentin peninsula.

He is, he declares, on a similar mission himself. Producing a large notepad, he explains that he has been collating a comprehensive survey of all cemeteries in the area, and just today discovered an interesting 15th-century charnel-house alongside a church on the outskirts of Valognes. He suggests that an illustrated guide to the graveyards and mausoleums of the Cotentin would be a popular addition to our guide, and offers his services as tour manager.

The idea of helping with our project draws immediate interest from the debating society at the bar, and soon I am offered all sorts of additional proposals for exposing the varied attractions of the Cotentin. Pierrot the Younger suggests organised hunting parties for school trips with guaranteed kills on every occasion, while Maurice Red-Nose staggers over to propose what at first appears to be a listing of all significant water features in the area. As Maurice is a prodigious toper and the morning is already well advanced, his patois is even more impenetrable than usual, but Freddo translates and I realise that rather than a guide to local waterfalls, Maurice is suggesting a guided tour to the places where he has measured his length while visiting secret stills and manufacturing centres for illicitly brewed calvados. He is also suggesting that I accompany him on his return visit to Maurice's Great Falls Around The Cotentin. He is quite happy to offer his services as guide and expert commentator for no fee, as long as I will take responsibility for all transport costs, and of course, the charge for all the products we shall need to sample and evaluate.

Before I become too interested, my wife points out that, quite apart from the ferry company's overview, it is hardly likely that the official local producers of calvados would appreciate the inclusion of a guide on exactly where to buy the best moonshine apple brandy in the whole of Normandy.

*   *   *   *   *

As we coast down the winding road towards the bay of Cherbourg, I enjoy the panaromic views of the ancient town and the English Channel beyond, and wonder once again why so many visitors seem so anxious not to linger in this pleasant and historic place.

Every year, hordes of British holidaymakers roll off the ferry boats and make straight for the main route south. As with so many old towns, the sprawling modern outskirts of Cherbourg hide its secret treasures like a golden nugget inside a lump of unremarkable stone, and all the fleeing visitors will see are the lines of box-like warehouses and discount stores alongside the *Route Nationale*. If they were to take a little time to visit the old town of Cherbourg, they would discover some much more interesting architecture.

Radiating from the market square, there are miles of narrow alleyways and shopping lanes where the old lives happily if sometimes disconcertingly alongside the new. Exploring a time-worn winding stone stairway in the old quarter, you are quite likely to come across a magnificent 16th-century hand-carved door which someone has decided to paint bright orange and festoon with electric bell-pushes. Near by will be a noble house frontage of interlocking slabs in local stone painstakingly dressed by a medieval mason, and now cheerfully punctuated with a row of plastic-framed and double-glazed windows.

This very French attitude to living unpretentiously with the past would doubtless give a British planning officer or architectural heritage enthusiast a seizure. To us, it is another refreshing example of the essential differences in attitude between our two cultures.

During the next two hours, we wander round the town, then take our ease at the public gardens to watch the seals being fed and old men in berets squabbling good-naturedly over long-running *boules* tournaments that only death will end.

In the *école des beaux arts*, we tour an exhibition of modern symbolism, and I enthuse over a carefully arranged pile of local stone. It obviously represents, I say, the rugged charms of this area, and I am about to ask the curator for his interpretation when a workman appears and wheelbarrows the stones away to continue the ongoing restoration work elsewhere in the building.

Returning to the maze of alleyways in the heart of the old town we decide to rest for lunch, and in a narrow passage between a used moped centre and a very expensive lingerie boutique, we find a restaurant which is entirely in keeping with its surroundings.

Buffalo Billy's Burger Bar, Pool Room and Crêperie Salon proves to be as classic an example of the French flair for mixing style, design and standards as the day-glow medieval door we saw earlier.

In the window, there are a number of photographs showing teams of serious-looking young men in waistcoats, bow ties and, for some obscure reason, driving gloves. They are taking part in what the caption tells us is an English Pools competition. Alongside the entrance, a dispassionate wooden Red Indian holding a pool cue instead of a tomahawk stands guard.

Just inside the door, a large and heavily tattooed man is contentedly pulling at an evil-smelling cigar as he crafts a batch of wafer-thin *crêpes* over the wood fire crackling merrily below an obviously broken smoke detector. As he works, his dog obligingly helps satisfy the local health and hygiene canons by cleaning up the spillage from bowl to pan.

At the far end of the dimly-lit bar, a row of tables are keeping the English Pools enthusiasts busy, and at the bar, an elegant young woman in designer clothing is having a fight to the death with a monstrous baguette stuffed with chips, fried eggs and slices of hamburger, all annointed with what looks to be a very good quality salad dressing.

In the neutral zone between bar and sports room, a cluster of chairs and tables are grouped conveniently close to the single toilet, and are mostly occupied by smartly dressed businessmen who are clearly enjoying their fine wines and *crêpes*. The walls behind the diners are lined with paintings and photographs of assorted native American tribe members setting about hapless pioneers, and from the ceiling hangs a collection of tomahawks, lances and other western memorabilia.

We take a table immediately below an interesting collection of realistic-looking scalps, and place our order with a waitress in full warpaint and feathered head-dress. As the thud of recorded drums and chants competes with the measured click of billiard balls and polite applause for a particularly skilful shot, I visit the unisex toilet and make a mental note to add it to my list for the book I will one day write about unusual and classic conveniences in the Cotentin. This example is of the very traditional no-nonsense hole-in-the ground variety, but without the traditional and often essential straining bars at crouched waist level. As I zip up and prepare to leave, I come face to face with the pretty waitress, who smiles and squeezes past as we make polite conversation about the clement weather, and I am immediately reminded of an unfortunate incident during a recent visit to England. Deep in thought while taking a break at a motorway stop, I wandered into the nearest toilet entrance and smiled politely at a young woman who was leaving one of the adjoining cubicles. Outside, I was detained by a security guard and the manager of the complex, and it took some time to convince them that, where I lived, it was quite normal to share toilet facilities.

After a superb meal, I begin to make notes for our guide book, but my wife reminds me of my concern that publicising some of the area's secret treasures may spoil them, and that anyway, while having real appeal to the locals and outsiders like us, Buffalo Billy's may not be to the taste of the typical British visitor.

I agree, whoop for the waitress, and order a large Sitting Bull Sundae to go with our bottle of perfectly chilled Sauvignon '93.

*   *   *   *   *

Outside, our mood of contentment evaporates as we find a large and ominously official-looking envelope stuck on Victor's windscreen. At first I think it is a parking ticket, then see that the letter inside concerns a recent prohibition on cars smoking while in Cherbourg.

In recent years there has been an increasing drive to ban smoking in public places, but as it has been totally ignored throughout our area and the rest of France, a bid to stop motorists enjoying a cigarette while driving seems highly optimistic. On our way into the town I had noticed a poster declaring that drink and driving equals death, and say to Donella that I hope the penalty for smoking in one's own car will not be as draconian. Looking more closely at the jargonised letter, I realise it is Victor who is the culprit. The text says he has recently been observed emitting dense clouds of white smoke, and is probably contributing more to the pollution of the town's environment than a fleet of juggernauts. This time, the letter ends, it is a friendly warning, but in future our car is liable to be arrested and taken away for enforced tests.

I tear the letter into pieces, but agree with my wife that Victor has not been well of late. Over the past decades he has carried many tons of building materials and furniture across the Channel and to all points of the peninsula. Without a complaint, he has ferried garden supplies, whole trees and even the odd goat around the area. Now it seems even he is nearing the end of his personal road through life. I had noticed the increasing volume of thick white smoke from the exhaust, but put it down to absent-mindedly filling the tank with two-stroke moped mixture at the garage at Néhou after my last visit to a particularly long and arduous Jolly Boys meeting.

We discuss the situation as I drive carefully away from Buffalo Billy's, and I agree it is time for Victor to go in for a full check-up and any remedial treatment required. I am not normally a sentimentalist when it comes to inanimate objects, but Victor the Volvo has been a faithful servant for many a year, and is now almost one of the family.

*   *   *   *   *

We have made our pilgrimage to Utah Beach, and it has been a poignant and sobering experience.

The scene of the first American attack during the D-Day invasion, the beach is on the eastern side of the peninsula, where the even coastline and low tidal rise gave the Allied troops their best chance of a successful landing. Nowadays it is a most tranquil place to be, but reminders of the savagery which took place along the shore on the 6th of June, 1944, are all around us.

The ranks of barbed wire and wicked metal stakes have long since gone, and the abandoned gun emplacements now lay mostly buried in the bone-white sand. But surrounding the museum and memorial, a number of strangely archaic-looking engines of war lay scattered amongst the shallow dunes. Rather than being restored and scrupulously maintained as would happen in Britain, the rusting tanks and cannon appear to have been left where and as they were immediately after the battle, which seems somehow much more fitting as a stark example of what horrors happened here in relatively recent times.

Leaving the car park, we walked up to the brow, and looked out at the calm waters, trying to imagine what it must have been like for both armies as the time for engagement drew near. Beyond the horizon, hundreds of tiny landing craft would be bouncing across the waves, carrying frightened young men, some of whom would never before have travelled a hundred miles from their homes or even seen the sea.

After five miserable days crossing the Atlantic on a troop ship, they would have been confined to a muddy, rain soaked camp near the English coast, waiting for the order which would send them to fight and perhaps die in someone else's war. Then, when the order came, they would have spent endless hours tossed around on the grey and heaving waters of the English Channel, far from home, desperately weary, seasick and fearful as the moment to scramble ashore under a hail of fire approached. For many, death must have been almost a release.

On the shore and awaiting the invasion would not be a crack division of battle-hardened stormtroopers, but a makeshift army of young and elderly conscripts, dragged from their homes across Germany to kill people with whom they had no quarrel. On this peaceful day, I stood on the remains of a pill-box and tried to think how someone just like my son would feel to be here, wearing a rough and ill-fitting uniform, clutching his rifle with a pounding heart and dry mouth and trying not to show his terror as the sky became black with warplanes and the greatest armada in history rose slowly over the horizon. Then would come the hell of noise and screaming and explosion, with fear spurring inhumanities beyond the imaginings of those who have never had to fight for their lives.

With my privileged life and limited imagination, it was, of course, impossible to fully appreciate what it would be like to have to risk leaving your life upon a distant beach so that other people might be free. Even so, it is a debt that our and future generations will never be able to repay, and should never forget.

*   *   *   *   *

Leaving the silent beach to its memories, we decide to take the backroads to home, and my wife recalls a visit to La Puce by an elderly friend and Normandy veteran on the 50th anniversary of the Landings. As a young Royal Marine bandsman in 1944, he had fought at Avranche, and wanted to return once more before it was too late.

As we retraced his journey of fifty years before, he had told us how his drum had been taken away and replaced with a rifle he hardly knew how to use. With the landing craft nearing the hostile shore, he had asked a sergeant for help and been brusquely advised just to point his gun at the men with the funny-shaped helmets and pull the trigger. It was only after several days of fierce fighting that our friend noticed how similar were the shapes of the German and the American helmets.

Hopefully, he said, he had picked the right targets; but anyway he was sure he had shot most of his bullets in the air.

During our conversation we have become lost and I stop to ask a farmer the best way to the RN13. He tells us we should go through the village of mad dogs, then looks at Victor's battered body, smiles knowingly and says we at least should be safe. Mystified, we drive on and eventually arrive at the village of St-Pierre-du-Val, where a huge gothic cathedral sits on a grassy knoll, surrounded by a huddle of houses, a garage and a café.

As we navigate the narrow road around the cathedral, we are pursued by a pack of yelping dogs led by a Jack Russell with a noticeable limp. Pulling up, we park and race for cover and they lose interest and disappear in search of other prey.

In the bar, the patron apologises and tells us a strange story. Nobody in the village knows why, but it has become a tradition for the local dogs to chase visiting cars. Their leader is a small but particularly ferocious English terrier known as Mad Max, and the pack only attacks new cars, and especially those bearing Paris number plates. It is a complete mystery, he concludes as he serves our coffee and winks at a customer with grease-stained hands and an even greasier set of overalls. The man finishes his *pastis*, and we watch as he leaves and walks across the road towards the garage.

As he enters the workshop, he whistles sharply, and the Jack Russell limps into view.

Wagging his stump of a tail, Mad Max settles down to watch his master restoring the bodywork of a stylish new car with Parisian number plates and a long series of ugly scratches on it shiny flank.

*   *   *   *   *

Trundling smokily down the track to the cottage of the Flea, we find that Postman Patrice has paid us a visit and left our mail in the woodshed. He has also left a note reminding me of the long-standing invitation to a *soirée* at his home, and stressing how much Madame is looking forward to meeting me. He adds that his operation will take place next week so we will not be seeing him for some time as he will be recuperating at the hospital for at least a month. Reading between the lines, our postman sounds almost pleased to be away from home for such a lengthy period.

Inside the cottage, we divide up the day's post, and I am pleased to see we have another bulletin and recipe from a distant friend and personal mentor.

Neville Palmer is a man with very short legs and a brain and soul as big as a very big planet. A sage, philosopher and satisfyingly incompetent tile grouter, the former head teacher has lived in the Dordogne with his wife Eve since retirement, and they are patently happy to have made the choice of starting a new adventure in the full summer of their years.

Nev is a man who has obviously found what he is looking for, and his philosophy is based broadly on a couplet he sent me after I had besieged him with my fears, frustrations and worries for the future when things were not going as planned at the Mill of the Flea. It simply read: *Grow bold along with me, the next is yet to be.*

My contemplative friend writes now and then when the mood takes him, and his letters are a joy as he describes the steady lack of progress on the makeover on their house, the much more important and loving creation of a wondrous garden, and the growth of his waistline in tandem with his exploration of the delights of the table in his part of France.

His latest bulletin ranges over the juciest gossip in the village, the blooming of the garden, and his recent gastronomic and gastropodic adventures.

Dispensing with domestic developments after promising that he is almost ready to put the last tile in the bathroom after two years of distractions elsewhere, Nev goes on to describe a recent foray to his local town of Ribérac, and I quickly decide to hide the letter before Donella sees it. Ribérac is said (by the Ribéracois) to be France's capital of *foie gras* production, and Nev devotes some time to describing most graphically the daily *gavage*, when kilos of maize are funnel-fed down the willing throats of geese in order to swell their livers and create the most expensive potted meats in the world. As he comments almost wistfully, larks' tongues were once even more of a luxury item in his area, but nowadays, it is hard to find the larks.

Commenting on my letter about the misunderstanding over the chickens' supper during our recent visit to the home of Aristide Goulet, my friend recalls an interesting experience from his early days in the Dordogne. In such a green and fertile region, sun and rain are equally abundant, and he was puzzled by the appearance in his neighbourhood of local people scouring ditches with buckets after every downpour. Investigation revealed that his neighbours were in search of snails, not water.

I turn to Nev's mouth-watering recipe for the preparation, cooking and enjoyment of what Périgordins call *cagouilles* and another Big Idea for making a living from the natural resources of our land arrives like a cartoon light bulb over my head. In the Cotentin, rain is never in short supply, and battalions of snails enjoy the fruits of my wife's vegetable garden more than we do.

Secreting the letter down the back of an armchair, I pull on my wellington boots and go in search of a bucket and butterfly net. Officially, the snails at La Puce may not be of the edible variety, but in my experience, that has never stopped a true Frenchman from eating anything that moves, however slowly.

Repas Palmer

To start: Duck Soup

The monstrous birds in our area are capable of feeding six people with equally big appetites, and each one will provide litres of fat for fried potatoes and other health foods. The stripped carcass can be bought at market for pennies, and here's how to put the last remains to good use:

Ingredients (for lots of people)

One large duck carcass
3 potatoes
Half a celeriac
3 slim leeks
A small and firm white cabbage
Some thin slices of wholemeal bread
Some salt, four cloves, a couple of bay leaves and around three litres of water

50g dried, white haricot beans
2 onions
A small turnip
3 sticks of celery

Method

Put the beans, the onions, cloves and bay leaves with the broken-up carcass in a commodious saucepan and cover with water. Bring to the boil, season according to your doctor and conscience, and simmer for two hours. Then strain. In the meantime, you will have peeled the other vegetables, holding back the cabbage for the time being. Cut the rest into generous chunks and add to the simmering stock. At almost the same time, cut your cabbage into four quarters, blanch them in boiling water for five minutes, then add the pieces to the soup. Now, you cook and wait. After around an hour and when the ingredients have shared their tastes, all you have to do is line your bowls with the bread, spoon the soup over, and enjoy.

Second course: *Terrine de Campagne*

Ingredients

1 kilo of belly pork
Some thin strips of pork fat
2 rounded tablespoons of flour
A liqueur glass of brandy
Half an onion

350g pig's liver
2 eggs
50g double cream
2 large cloves of garlic

You will also require a bay leaf, thyme, a generous serving of chopped parsley and some salt and pepper.

Method

Roughly mince together the belly pork, liver, onion, peeled garlic and parsley. Add the brandy, salt and pepper. Leave the lot in the fridge overnight. The next day, mix the eggs, lightly beaten, with the cream and the flour and blend into the pork mixture. Pile it all into a terrine dish lined with the strips of fat, put the thyme and the bay leaf on top of the meat mixture and fold the ends of the fat over the top. The next bit sounds complicated, but isn't. Mix a simple stiff flour and water paste and use it to seal the terrine lid. Put the dish into a bain-marie (or just a larger casserole with water halfway up the sides of the terrine) and cook for two hours in an oven set at gas 5 or 6. Leave it alone in a cool place for at least twenty four hours, and preferably three or four days before serving. Kept cool, your terrine will last for up to eight days (if you allow it to survive that long!).

Main course: *Cagouilles à la Jacqueline*

First, as they say, catch your snails, or as Ribéracois say, your *cagouilles*. If you lived in our area, you would by now have set up your own snail farm, feeding your charges on lush lettuce leaves until their gastropodic feet swell way beyond the back of their shells. This would be followed by days and days of cleansing by feeding the unsuspecting snails on wholesome fodder before a fast, and the total evacuation of their bowels of what the French call *crotte*, and we call crud. Then would come a lengthy simmering in court bouillon, after which each snail would be removed from its home and set aside while the shells are boiled again for complete sterilisation. While all this is going on, you would be preparing your stuffing of chopped ham and breadcrumbs and garlic and parsley and herbs and butter and seasoning and one or two other very local and personal secret ingredients. Then it would be time to artfully refit each mollusc into its original and now shining case, stopping up the exit with the stuffing. Your *cagouilles* would then at last be laid out in baking dishes (at least fifty snails per guest in our circles), annointed with butter and finished off in a hot oven.

As you may not be in a position to set up your own snail farm, why not take the easy way out and buy some, complete with shells and stuffing and ready to heat up? This is the ultimate in convenience food, and you may just be lucky enough to find some from Ribérac. The ones you buy in supermarkets on both sides of the Channel will be stuffed with parsley butter. They are far from the real thing, but give at least a flavour of what good eating the humble snail can make. Lastly on the subject: although I love George dearly, I cannot in all heart recommend that you settle for snails from La Puce, however well prepared and stuffed...

Afters: *Tarte à la Citrouille*

Each autumn, the market is full of different shapes and types of pumpkin (*citrouille*) and other squashes. Although outsiders might argue that pumpkin pie is quintessentially American, I am assured that our local version was being enjoyed here long before the *Mayflower* even set sail from Plymouth. Perhaps it's another example, as our residents would say, of foreigners taking a classic French regional dish and claiming it for their own.

Ingredients

Enough short-crust pastry to line a medium sized flan dish
Around 350g of the flesh from your *citrouille*
Four eggs   225g of granulated sugar
About 15g (two tablespoons) flour   Approximately 40g butter
A generous sprinkling (about half a teaspoon) of cinnamon
A pinch each of ground allspice and ground ginger
125ml (quarter pint) cream

Method

Chop up your *citrouille* flesh, steam and rub through a sieve. Line your flan dish with the pastry and blind bake (pricked well, the bottom covered with foil spread with baking beans) for 20 minutes at gas mark 6 (200°C). Mix the purée with the egg yolks, flour, spices, sugar, cream and melted butter. Whip the egg whites with a little salt until they are stiff but still quite soft, and fold into the pumpkin mixture. Pour into the pastry case and cook for about 50 minutes at gas mark 3 (170°C). Serve hot, or cold with cream.

As to drinks with this meal, there's a lovely custom in our area. Neither wine nor extra bread are taken with soup. Instead, when the dish is empty, you put your spoon into it with the bowl up, then fill the dish up to the bowl of the spoon with red wine. Invariably, the wine will be the produce of a local farmer at four or five francs a bottle. Swish the wine round to soak up the juices and drink it, and you will have followed the old Occitan custom where you *faire lou chabrol.*

For the terrine, you might go upmarket with Bergerac *rouge*, fruity but with just enough tannin to cut the rich pork mixture.

With the main course, perhaps a Côtes de Duras *blanc*, the favourite wine of the 16th-century King Francis I. With the pudding, I would recommend a Monbazillac, sweet and local, and the regular choice with *pâté de foie gras*.

Then the *digestif*. George enthuses about his Cotentin applejack *calva*, but it's not a patch on *Eau de vie de prunes*, which is our local head-banger. We grow a lot of plums, and even my little garden produces about 100 kilos. What happens is that all the fruit, windfalls and all, are gathered and kept in a large barrel or several plastic dustbins. Then, in the autumn, the peripatetic distiller, complete with wood-burning distillation engine, turns up and camps on commune land by the stream. The locals bring their collection of ageing plums and distillation produces a special plum brandy. After this, by mystic processes, sometimes a liqueur of 80-100 per cent proof emerges. As the old poet almost said, "Sip gently, or taste not the Empyrean spring."

Local knowledge

As one who long in populous city pent
Where houses thick and sewers annoy the air
Forth issuing on a summers morn to breathe
Amongst the pleasant villages and farms
Adjoined, from each thing met conceives delight.

Milton, *Paradise Lost*

Dusk steals gently across the water meadow, and all is abloom at the Mill of the Flea.

We are in the midst of a glorious summer, and it is our custom to spend long hours beside the big pond after the day's labours. This afternoon, Donella repaired the gate to the mill garden, weeded the vegetable patch, cleared out a blocked sewage pipe and laid out row after row of wire fencing upon which to support her new vineyard. Meanwhile, I had been called to attend a special meeting of the Jolly Boys Club and cast my vote on a motion to purchase a mobile telephone on special offer from Dodgy Didier. The proposal was to equip the JBC with the means of instant communication should important club matters or emergencies arise, but the motion (unsurprisingly moved by Didier) was defeated after some hours of thoughtful discussion. Apart from the members agreeing that they could think of no emergency warranting the scandalous cost of a call, the fact that it would be difficult to have a two-way conversation with only one telephone between us made the project a non-starter.

Now, my wife and I are enjoying the end of another busy day with a glass of cider, and many of the residents of the pond have joined us in taking the evening air. The arch-beast has not yet appeared, so the other creatures are making the most of the opportunity to celebrate surviving another day in their short but eventful lives.

This year's massed squadrons of emperor, dragon and damselflies are as usual totally sex-obsessed, and clumsily coupling up in midair like refuelling aeroplanes with drunken pilots at the controls. As ever, they are blissfully unaware of Triple Salco and his troupe of performing frogs, many of whom are crouching on the tips of flag irises at the water's edge, waiting for a suitable opportunity to launch themselves in search of high tea.

Emboldened by the muskrat's absence, a brace of water voles have ventured out from beneath the upturned dinghy to take the evening air, and a sinister waving of claws just above the murky surface of the pond signals that the surviving members of the crayfish gang are out and about and looking for trouble.

Even our pair of reclusive muscovy ducks have emerged from the safety of the long grass and are paddling happily around the pond's central island. As I relax and ruminate on the pleasures of a simple life, my wife is perfecting her technique of sending slices of sandwich bread skimming across the pond to a favourite fish, and we are amused to see Triple Salco leap from his observation post on to a large crust. Croaking contentedly, he settles down on his artificial lily pad to contemplate a friendly race between a couple of tiny water boatman, but soon discovers he has made a serious tactical mistake. Within moments, at least a dozen warriors of the Psycho tribe have surrounded his flimsy vessel and begun to eat the bread away from the outside edges. The force of their attack sends the slice spinning crazily around the island as it diminishes rapidly in size, and our frog commander looks for all the world like a doomed mariner adrift on a raft in a sea of sharks.

Donella appears nearly as distressed by the situation as he does, and orders me to dive in and rescue him. I refuse on the grounds that I am not prepared to make the ultimate sacrifice and expose myself to the frenzied goldfish for the sake of a single frog, but show willing by lobbing a sizeable lump of stone at the melee. The stone hits the bread, which breaks into a dozen pieces, and Triple Salco makes good his escape in the confusion as the predators turn on each other in their frenzy to bag the biggest portions of debris.

Peace eventually returns to the big pond, then a distant hoot signals the lateness of the hour, and the inmates scatter to the safety of their holes, burrows and nests like Transylvanian villagers fleeing the terrors of the approaching night.

We sit in the gathering gloom as the first flight of noctule bats wheel and circle overhead, then something stirs in the long grass by the jetty. It is time for the muskrat to start his nightly prowl in search of victims, and the other residents of the big pond have no desire to be dinner guests of the big pond's Prince of Darkness.

*   *   *   *   *

It is after eleven o'clock, and we too are safely indoors at the mill cottage. Cato the werecat has slipped out to join his fellow creatures of the night, and I am just settling down to catch up on my latest correspondence from friends across France when my wife announces that we have visitors.

As the murmur of voices outside becomes louder, I slump in my chair and pretend to be asleep, but no knock at the door signals the arrival of friendly callers. Eventually, I am persuaded by my wife that we should confront the nocturnal trespassers, and taking the shotgun with the missing trigger from above the stove, I follow her out on to the terrace.

It is a cloudless night and a million stars have turned night into day, but there is no sign of human presence. We stand, straining our ears, and hear further sounds of conversation coming from the direction of the water meadow. My heart in my mouth and my useless gun levelled, I reluctantly creep around the corner of the cottage, to find no poachers, but a sea of disembodied voices all round me.

As I turn to flee, I recognise the measured tones of a news reader giving the latest share prices on the Dow Jones index and the mystery is solved. Though the lines of taut wire in my wife's vineyard have as yet to bear fruit, they are obviously perfect receivers of radio waves, and the residents of the water meadow will now be able to keep up with events abroad courtesy of the BBC World Service.

*   *   *   *   *

A glorious morning, and I am particularly excited today as we are about to be launched upon the international super highway of communication. At least, if all goes well we will be able to watch the telly this evening.

Over the years at the Mill of the Flea, we have experimented with all sorts of ways of keeping in visual touch with what is happening elsewhere in France and the rest of the world. As one of Old Pierrot's pet crows flies, Jersey is no more than thirty miles away and the island has a relay station which transmits all terrestrial British TV channels. Should they choose, expatriot settlers and Normans with the right sort of television set can tune in daily to the histrionic goings-on in our soap operas, or watch teams of demented and bossy 'stylists' invade innocent family homes to transform their living rooms or gardens into no-go areas. This is obviously a strong contributing factor as to why so many of our villagers think that all English people are sad, mad or both.

At La Puce, we have been shielded from the dumbing-down of British TV, and are frequently reminded by bemused neighbours how lucky we are to have escaped from a society which is obviously on the brink of collapse through unrealistic and unremitting self-regard. We are immune to the Channel Island transmissions as the mill cottage at La Puce was sensibly built at the lowest point in the area so water would run past it, which also means we are unable to receive French television. According to those of our British friends who can tune in, this is also no bad thing. But I have to confess that I miss the opportunity to wallow in the odd re-run of *Dad's Army* or a thrilling snooker tournament.

To be honest, along with hard cheese, real pubs, baked beans and proper sandwich bread, there are a number of things I miss about the English way of life, and one of them is the ability to look at the odd programme worth watching. In my weaker moments, I even long for a quick fix of *Countdown*. The radio gives us all the news we want, but it is a test match year, so I have taken steps to ensure I will be able to see England thrashed by the opposition.

Though I should know better by now, I have done a deal with Didier, the travelling salesman and general dealer who visits Néhou every week. Didier is said to live in Cherbourg, though nobody knows exactly where, and makes his living by peddling a bewildering variety of goods around the hinterland. Few work or have any practical application to the average rural Norman, but all have the advantage of being very cheap. It is said that Dodgy Didier is able to offer such bargain prices by shortening the retail chain and buying direct from the back of the endless stream of lorries passing through the dock gates at Cherbourg. The drawback is that his bargain buys invariably fail to provide their basic function and his promise. But somehow, he always seems to find a ready market, even for the most obscure items. Last year, he was offering a special line in blank Rubik's cubes, and the amazing thing was that hundreds of people bought one, including me. Like all successful dealers, Didier has a nose for a sucker, and he knows that I in common with so many others will buy anything providing I think I am getting a bargain. Sometimes, I know he actually buys his goods legitimately but pretends they are stolen to give them more appeal and explain the low price.

This time, however, he has promised me he has the answer to my communication problems. He has, he claims, cornered the market in a revolutionary new digital satellite dish. As I will be his first customer in the area and a good advertisement for future sales, he will even throw in a marvellous television set which can be adjusted to receive English, French and every other wavelength I may care to tune in to. It is the type used by the American Armed Forces, and absolutely the latest thing in technological advancement.

Despite my better judgement and past brushes with Dodgy Didier, I am excited at the prospect of seeing as well as hearing the cricket this year. At the last Jolly Boys meeting I handed over a thick wad of five hundred franc notes, and as René Ribet has been appointed as Didier's installation executive for this area, our friend will be arriving this morning to fit the dish on the roof. In an hour, I will be hooked up and plugged in, and can spend the summer watching the uniquely English game which, as Didier says, nobody else in the world understands but all can beat us at. I have not told Donella how much the equipment cost, but she is looking forward to a feast of nature programmes. In anticipation, I have bought a satellite TV guide for the month so I can plan our viewing. I have also made a mental note to avoid the late-night horror films as I don't want Cato getting any ideas from tonight's classic, which is a special screening of *The Curse of the Werewolf.*

*   *   *   *   *

Our attempt to become part of the digital revolution has not been wholly successful. Early doubts surfaced when René Ribet wobbled down the track on his moped with the satellite dish strapped to his back and the rest of my expensive and delicate receiving equipment stacked in the general purpose trailer he hitches to his moped when there are any heavy moving jobs to be done.

For such a sophisticated piece of equipment, the dish looked remarkably like a dustbin lid painted black, but he assured me he had unpacked it from the box with his own hands, and waved the installation instructions as proof. Unfortunately, the manufacturers had not thought to include English or Normandy French amongst the variety of languages in the brochure, but René assured me it was all common sense.

I was also disappointed with the all-purpose television set. The screen was square and very small, and the khaki-coloured box looked more like something left over from the D-Day landings rather than the latest development in communications technology.

Before starting work, we had the obligatory drinks session to help with his sense of balance, then The Fox swarmed up the ladder and disappeared behind the chimney pot. All went well for a few moments, till I heard a chilling yowl and a muffled curse,

109

and had to take evasive action to avoid a shower of roofing tiles. Climbing the ladder and peering cautiously over the ridge, I found that René had met our werecat for the first time. Blood had been drawn and I shall have to see if my friend acts oddly as the time for full moon approaches, though it could be hard to tell the difference from his normal behaviour. A positive outcome from the encounter is that René is sure to tell of his encounter with Cato, and the tale will more than probably grow with the telling. I shall look forward to the arrival of hunters from all across the region, armed to the teeth and eager to get to grips with the Beast of La Puce.

Apart from the lacerations, our unofficial estate manager seemed none the worse for the experience; in fact, he seemed quite pleased with the collateral damage to the roof, as he is in charge of all repairs and maintenance at the Mill of the Flea.

After a break for some basic first aid and another couple of drinks, René returned to the roof and, before long, all was ready for La Puce to join the digital communications revolution. Following a short address, I pressed a random selection of buttons on the front of the set, and we sat back to enjoy the show. As if by magic, a crystal-clear picture appeared almost immediately, and I at first thought we were watching a re-run of *Lawrence of Arabia*.

After clicking through a selection of channels, all apparently presented by the same man wearing an ill-fitting wig and orange makeup and talking very quickly in a very foreign tongue, we concluded that Didier had obtained his consignment from a lorry passing through Cherbourg en route to the Middle East.

Following another round of drinks, René helped me compose an advertisement for the local free sheet, offering any Arabic-speaking readers a real bargain, and I settled for listening to the next Test match on our vineyard radio.

*　　*　　*　　*　　*

Donella is increasingly worried about Victor's health, so we are off for a consultation with a local specialist.

In an idle moment recently, I calculated that our trusty estate car has transported us and more than twenty tons of assorted payload a distance of around a quarter of a million miles since Donella rescued him from an uncaring former owner. The exact mileage is uncertain as the speedometer has not worked for some years, and we tend to judge our speed by the rattle factor and how fast trees and road signs seem to be going past. What is certain is that Victor has crossed and re-crossed the Channel more times than some ferry boats, been in the strangest of places and situations, and apart from packhorse and means of general transport, has doubled as an office, bedroom, dining room and, on one memorable occasion, the venue for a cocktail party. We have shared countless experiences together, and he has never let us down.

Now, I fear he is reaching the end of his usefulness, but my wife is prepared to go to any expense to maintain his quality of life. The money we have spent on repairs in recent years would have bought a much newer model, but my wife will not even discuss trading him in. Whatever it costs, she says, Victor must have the necessary medical treatment, even if it means a full transplant of all his most vital organs.

*   *   *   *   *

A moving cloud, we leave the mill track and limp along the D900 to the crossroads leading to our village. St Georges de Néhou is the proper name of the commune, but the inhabitants never use it. Convenience is generally claimed to be the reason, but I suspect it is because the full title of our rival village on the other side of the main road is St Jacques de Néhou, and in France, St Jacques is a far more important saint than St Georges. He was also, apparently, a much better cook.

In appearance, our Néhou is like a hundred other villages in Normandy, and probably throughout rural France, consisting mainly of a gaggle of houses, a church, school, bar and shop and garage. As with any community, though, its true identity lies in its people rather than in what it looks like. In our commune, there is said to be a population of around three hundred, but nobody has bothered to do a proper head count for a number of years.

Coughing and spluttering, Victor struggles along the winding uphill approach to the village, passing by a patchwork of lush fields from which cows stare incuriously at the low-lying cloud in which we sit.

The first sign of habitation is our local *manoir*, with its ornate arched gateway and impressive facade contrasting oddly with the muddy yard and its jumble of farm implements, old cars and huge sileage clamp that is destined to become, if René Ribet has his way, the Néhou Millennium Dome. As we pass the yard, a farmhand with his head and shoulders in the innards of an ancient tractor stands up and peers with narrowed eyes in our direction. He is obviously trying to identify us through the masking pall of smoke, and we know that any passing car would be carefully logged for later reporting to the local intelligence pool. Within an hour or so, everyone in the village will know that we have been on a visit, that Victor is sick, what we are wearing today, what we bought in the grocery shop and how much to the centilitre I drank during our stay.

To some, this tracking and data-collecting system might seem intrusive, but it is part of the price one pays for a virtually crime-free society and we are more than happy to pay it. The official crime rate in and around Néhou is as near to zero as it can be, and this may well have more to do with people knowing they are under permanent scrutiny than some sort of honesty gene peculiar to country people living in small and isolated communities.

Soon, we are bumping over the long-dead railway line and past the village school, with its colourful rows of geraniums lining the low wall and the *tricolor* proudly flying from the gatepost. Inside, neatly dressed children will be having their lessons, and there will not be a single mobile phone between them. When the school day is over, there will be no log-jam of cars bearing anxious mothers queuing to pick their precious offspring up, and no drug dealers or perverts lying in wait as the pupils walk home.

After school, the building becomes the town hall, with our mayor sitting in judgement on a variety of local issues and making his decisions to ensure natural as well as official justice. The mayor is, of course, the central figure in any community; a good mayor can oil the wheels of bureaucracy, and at the same time pour liberal amounts of it on troubled waters. He can grant instant planning permission, and has other ways of avoiding potentially troublesome situations by turning a blind eye at the right time. With such a system there is always the risk of corruption, but nobody has yet thought of a better way of providing a practical figurehead for thousands of small and often isolated communities. There was a national outcry a few years ago when an English settler was elected as mayor of a village in the south, but in our area nothing that happens in that part of the country comes as much of a surprise. A mischievous member of the Jolly Boys Club used the incident as an excuse to propose that I run in the next election for mayor of Néhou, but the idea was so ridiculous that nobody even bothered to second it. As Old Pierrot observed, it will need at least a dozen gravestones in the churchyard with my family name on them before I am fit to be considered a real member of the commune, let alone a mayoral candidate. When a few generations have passed, he has said he will consider sponsoring a suitable descendant of mine. By that time, he reckons, the East family may have learned to speak the language of their adopted country properly.

Now we are approaching the home and office of our area policeman, and I see from the battered moped outside that he has not as yet been called out to investigate the disappearance of a pig or to mediate in a dispute over the ownership of a pile of logs.

Though he has a huge patch to patrol, our intemperate bobby

Claude Poivrot is not overworked. He has no radio, but when not at home can usually be found by ringing around the bars in the area. It is rumoured that he has a breathalyser as part of his crimefighting equipment, but said that he has not taken it with him since he tested it on himself and found he was miles above the legal limit at breakfast time, and even before the first drink of the day. It was obviously faulty, he reasoned, so it has remained in a drawer in his office ever since.

As we belch our way past the large field next to the village hall, I see that the building of Mr Junot's retirement home is nearing completion.

A distant neighbour of ours, the gentle giant with hands the size of small shovels and a moustache under which a small family could shelter from the rain is nearing the age when he must give up his farm, so is building his own house in which to enjoy the autumn of his life. It is in an elevated position with fine views across the surrounding countryside, and the clay soil will make a good foundation for the building. The site's most important quality, however, is that it is midway between the village hall and the Bar Ghislaine, so our amiable friend will not have far to walk for JBC meetings and to organise the drinks at village functions.

From what I can see through the enveloping cloud of smoke from Victor's rear, it appears that Mr Junot's new house will have a boiler and fuel tank big enough to heat the whole village. Then as a gust of wind improves visibility for a moment, I see that the two great vessels are actually oak casks in which hundreds of gallons of home-brew *calva* will now be gently maturing. Rather than having the problem of fitting the barrels into his new home, it seems our friend has taken the sensible step of building his house around them.

Onward we travel, and as the church and cemetery come into view, I see Ronald Dedman is working in the garden of his neat little cottage. As we draw abreast, I toot the horn and he looks up and waves. From his ghostly dust-powdered face and the hammer and chisel he is waving, he appears to be inscribing details on the large slab of marble propped on a kitchen chair. If it is his own gravestone he is making he has left it a little late, but at least he will be able to fill in his date of death rather than leaving it to someone else.

We are on the last leg of our journey through the village and into the heart of the Valley of Néhou, and I see from the line of cars, tractors and mopeds outside the Bar Ghislaine that there will be a full attendance at today's Jolly Boys Club meeting.

I also see that my friends have been warming up for the event, as there are five sets of broad shoulders jockeying for position at the *pissoir* next to the grocery store window. As we limp past, René Ribet turns to wave us on our way, and my wife scowls and averts her eyes as she realises that it is not his hand with which he is waving.

* * * * *

Victor has had his examination, and the prognosis is not good. The chief mechanic at the garage at Néhou is highly competent, but elderly foreign cars are not his forté, so we have been to see an allegedly specialist surgeon who operates from his house in a hamlet in the Valley of Néhou.

Unusually tall for a Norman, and with a permatan of engine oil and grease and the odd missing finger, Mr Bougie spent at least an hour delving into Victor's most private parts and I knew that the diagnosis would not be favourable from the expensive way he shrugged, shook his head, pursed his lips and gave vent to sorrowful sighs at regular intervals throughout the examination. Having finally emerged from Victor's insides, he replaced his greasy beret, lit a cigarette, scratched his jaw, took his teeth out and looked at them sorrowfully, then finally delivered the verdict. In layman's terms, he explained, Victor is a very sick car. The smoking is something to do with water getting from somewhere to somewhere it shouldn't be, and it will take a major operation

115

to correct the disorder. Even then, it is likely Victor will be an invalid for the rest of his life.

It was Mr Bougie's recommendation that we send our old friend to the scrapheap and buy a proper French car, a wide selection of which he just happened to have at the back of the premises. If we are not interested in buying another car from him, he can fix us up with a moped and trailer on permanent leaseback, or he has a vintage and therefore very valuable tractor available for rental. A sturdy French *mobylette* would be much cheaper to run and the trailer would be able to carry even more cargo than we have subjected our car to over the years. With the tractor, we would also have the added advantage of being able take the short cut from the bar at Néhou straight across fields, rivers and ditches to our home.

Despite the variety of options, Donella would not hear of investing in any new form of transport, and said that, whatever the cost, Victor must be made well again. This is a very dangerous instruction to give a Norman tradesman, and Mr Bougie brightened visibly as my wife told him to order all the necessary parts for Victor's operation and prepare for the vital transplant.

It was with a heavy heart we said goodbye to Mr Bougie and our car, and began the long walk to the Bar Ghislaine for today's JBC meeting. Donella is obviously worried about Victor's wellbeing, but I am more concerned about the cost of his operation and convalescence. Explaining that it is unlikely that he will find the right parts in the area and perhaps even in the whole of France, Mr Bougie's parting shot was that he would be quite prepared to fly to Sweden and pick them up personally.

*   *   *   *   *

We have arrived back at La Puce after a long and strange afternoon and evening, even by Néhou standards.

When we first moved over to settle at La Puce, the adjustment to the pace and idiosyncracies of village life took some time, but now I feel we have become almost fully acclimatised.

From one of the most densely populated cities in Britain, we found ourselves in a situation where our nearest neighbour was a quarter of a mile from our front door, and my wife and I were living on an area of land which would have been home to around three thousand people in Portsmouth. Donella took to the change of environment and circumstances instantly, but it has taken me some years to adapt.

In the early days, I would insist on driving to Cherbourg at least once a week just to be surrounded by people and cars and noise. Later, I found myself content to get my fix of big city life by visiting our local town of Bricquebec on a daily basis. Eventually I became used to the different disciplines and attractions of country living, and now we spend more and more time at La Puce, taking longer to do simple things and finding inordinate pleasure in small diversions and adventures. A trip to Néhou is now our idea of a journey to civilisation, and despite the tiny population, we find as much stimulation and interest in the goings-on in our commune as in any bustling metropolis.

I also find myself more at ease with my friends in the village than with many acquaintances in England. Here, people seem to judge a person by what is in his heart and not his pocket, nor by what he does for a living or what clothes he chooses to wear. Unless it is my imagination, it also seems that working people here and in other regions of France seem more ready to accept and even value those with creative aspirations or occupations. In JBC circles, it is not a matter for particular remark that the way I use my hands is different from theirs, and my working with words rather than a shovel is not a source of derision or suspicion as it might be in a circle of farmworkers in an English pub.

I suspect most of the people in the village think I am at least eccentric and probably slightly mad, but it is not a matter of great importance or a block to our friendship.

Today, the Bar Ghislaine was exceptionally busy, and our circle included an interesting overseas member.

Miguel Eduiz is of Portuguese extraction, lives in a caravan in a field just outside the village, and makes a patchy living rendering the fronts of local farm buildings in the style of his native land. He is a very short man with long arms and an almost completely flat face, both of which physical peculiarities he says are directly connected with his *métier*.

In his home country, he claims, it is the habit in families with a tradition of plastering to throw a new-born male child against the nearest wall. If the infant sticks fast to the heavily textured surface, he is obviously predestined to follow in his father's footsteps. If not, he will be schooled for some other trade. In Miguel's case, his long arms are a fortunate genetic coincidence, and a great saving as he doesn't have to waste money on tall ladders.

I don't know if he is joking as he is unable to keep anything else but a straight face, but he is a genial fellow and a fine tradesman. Naturally, my fellow members of the JBC find nothing unusual in Miguel's explanation for his looks, or the family tradition that allegedly gave him his most even of features. An outsider would doubtless think we are a strange crew, but we were shortly to be joined by a couple who made the most singular of our members appear quite normal.

As we debated the continuing issue of the proposed Millennium Silage Dome, the daylight from the bar window grew dim and an excited child rushed in to announce that a strange craft had landed in the street outside.

With barely a pause to make and carry the necessary motion, we moved our meeting out on to the pavement and saw that the alien vessel was a gigantic camper van, bigger than some of the cottages in the village, and probably containing more rooms and facilities. After a series of complicated docking manoeuvres and much hissing of air brakes and flashing lights, the vehicle came to rest and disgorged an exotic couple, one of whom looked as if she had been transported direct from a 1960's peace festival.

A tall, angular woman with sharp features and luminescent dark eyes, she was swathed in layers of clothing bearing more embroidery than the Bayeux Tapestry, and she was all a-jangle with rings, bangles and other body ornaments of the type found in craft shops where there are hundreds of painstakingly created home-made items but never any customers.

By comparison, her male companion looked almost normal. He was much shorter than her in spite of his platform boots, and more simply dressed in a Tibetan prayer bonnet, white safari jacket and jungle-friendly combat trousers of the type favoured by television reporters called to cover any story outside central London.

After breathing in the air like a ferret scenting a nearby rabbit colony, the woman made a beeline for our *pissoir*, then gave vent to a great sigh, which I at first took to be one of frustration. When I explained that, though we were not up to big city standards, there was a proper toilet for women in Madame Ghislaine's private quarters, she explained that the couple had arrived in search of spiritual rather than bodily relief.

Our outside convenience, it appears, straddles something called a ley line, and the exotic couple had been drawn by its mystic magnetism all the way from Cherbourg.

After tracing the line of unseen power to inside the bar, our visitors introduced themselves as Don and Peggy, though they prefer to be known by their former names of Osiris, the Ancient Egyptian deity of the fructification of the land, and Ra-Atum, who made his living in those times as the omnipotent and all-knowing sun god. In this life, they are based, unsurprisingly, in California. She is a painter and he is a sculptor, and they are travelling through France, looking for spiritual inspiration and suitable subjects for her next best-selling book containing sketches of people who once lived as well-known historical characters.

Within the hour, Mystic Peg had read the cosmic auras of all our circle and declared that René Ribet had once lived as the Bourbon Sun King, while Miguel the plasterer had discovered

119

America in his former incarnation as Vasco de Gama. Her own past lives have included Cleopatra, a brace of ancient Egyptian deities, Queen Boadicea of the Iceni, and more recently, a French woman who had given her life for the cause of the Resistance in World War II.

Brushing aside my observation of how strange it was that people who claim to have led past lives always seem to have been famous figures rather than chamber maids or pork butchers, Mystic Peg also correctly identified Old Pierrot as being an immortal. He was so pleased at this unsolicited confirmation of his claims that he offered to pose naked for a painting in her portfolio of Great Spirits of the Age of Aquarius.

After I had bought a round of drinks to celebrate the revelation that our *pissoir* is on the site of a pagan temple, the couple almost casually announced their intention of making Néhou a worldwide spiritual and healing centre. As Ra (by now we were all on first-name terms) explained while he borrowed my tobacco pouch, stuck three cigarette papers together and began to roll a curiously constructed and oversized cigarette, they had heard that the nearby *Château du Lude* is for sale, and were here to inspect it and make the mostly absentee Parisian owners an offer they would not be able to refuse.

Under their direction, the great building will be restored to its former glory, and at the same time become a refuge and what they called a centre of excellence to teach the very wealthy how to live with the burden of having great amounts of money. Having politely offered his giant roll-up to other members of our circle, Don/Ra-Atum took a deep draw, spluttered contentedly, then fleshed out the couple's vision.

Troubled souls with lots of money and too much time on their hands would, our visitors knew from experience, travel to our small village from all over the world for a period of reassessment of their lives and a healthy dose of spiritual instruction. The students would be fed on a wholesome and simple diet, and be encouraged to work in the fields of local farmers in order to help them appreciate the rewards of honest labour. Their time at

Néhou would help show them the triviality and complete unimportance of money when compared with a simple way of life and spiritual fulfilment. More than probably, said Osiris, many of these poor rich souls would want to dispossess themselves of the money which had proved such a blight on their lives.

A further attraction at the Néhou centre for spiritual enlightenment would be a special course on a new cult which has the bonus of relieving its followers of their weekly grocery bills. Started in Australia and now allegedly having millions of adherents around the world, the main proposition is that followers can exist solely by absorbing the power of the sun, and need never eat for the rest of their lives.

After their oversized cigarette had been offered around the circle again, the couple revealed what they called the bottom-line deal. To ensure participation and in order that everyone would be able to share in the material wealth the project would bring to the commune, the villagers would be allowed to invest in the buying and refurbishing of the *Château du Lude*. Shares would be made available, and, apart from the significant investment by Osiris and Ra, be limited to local people.

Having listened to the vision revealed by our visitors, I was saddened to see that my fellow members of the JBC seemed unable or unwilling to grasp the full potential of the project.

Although they obviously liked the idea of rich visitors bringing their money to Néhou and working in the fields for free, our membership was totally unwilling to even consider the idea of investing in shares. Old Pierrot was especially pessimistic about the proposed courses for learning to live without eating. He said he knew many people in the area who already survived on a diet of nothing more than a regular ingestion of *calva*, and besides, if it all hung on followers of the cult absorbing the life-giving energy of the sun, the weather in the Cotentin would ensure they would be kept on very short commons.

To be fair, I could understand why my friends were so sceptical

121

in spite of the relaxing nature of Ra's king-size cigarettes. In rural France, it is not unusual for strangers to arrive with grand schemes and ideas which they say will bring prosperity and change to the area; very often the proposals prove to have as little substance as the people who bring them. But after listening to Peg and Don's vision, I at least was full of enthusiasm for their plans and the part we might be allowed to play in them.

In spite of my wife's obvious antipathy, I invited our new friends back to La Puce for supper and continued discussions on their plans for the emergence of St Georges de Néhou as a spiritual centre of world renown.

*   *   *   *   *

It is well after midnight, and Osiris and Ra-Atum have finally settled down in their camper on the mill track next to the copse.

Before supper, they went on a mission to take the spiritual temperature of our land, and immediately identified the grotto as a place of eternal peace and contentment, and Donella's compost heap as being rich in the fecund forces of nature. They also brought back a handful of strangely shaped mushrooms which I had never seen in our copse, and shared some of Osiris's favourite recipes from her days as an Incan high priestess.

In spite of their obvious sincerity and even child-like innocence, Donella remained suspiciously aloof throughout the meal, and became even more distant when the couple invited us to be major shareholders in their spiritual centre. Leaving me to finish one of Ra's piquant cigarettes, Donella declared herself more than ready to retire, and escorted our guests to their camper without, I noticed, a word of warning that Cato the werecat might be on the prowl.

On her return, I also noticed that she double-locked the front door to our mill cottage for the first time since we moved to the Mill of the Flea, and for some reason made a point of telling me she had chained and padlocked the new cement mixer to the giant sycamore tree.

Given her mood, I thought it best not to tell her I had already made a small initial investment in the Néhou Temple of The Great Spirit by slipping Ra-Atum the emergency fund of cash money my wife keeps in the ornamental teapot on the mantelpiece.

Mystic Peg's Menu

These recipes for our meal with Ra-Atum and Osiris deliberately omit some of the key ingredients and substances they provided, as they are not only difficult to obtain in the average grocery shop, but in some cases are probably poisonous and perhaps even illegal. As far as I can remember, all the ingredients are of quantities to feed four people. Mind you, I also seem to remember we had a lot left over next morning.

To start: Nettle Soup

This is an ideal way to take advantage of the most prolific crop on any shady, dank and ill-managed piece of land. Apart from the natural reward of food for free, it is also very satisfying to get your own back on the source of so much summer discomfort by boiling the aggressors alive. In proper circles, it is said that you must only use the delicate new shoots at the top of the nettles, but we regularly use the whole plant chopped up and beaten senseless as a spinach substitute. Providing you use enough ferocity and lashings of butter and pepper, the result is healthily fibrous and surprisingly edible.

Author's disclaimer (1). A word of warning about the harvesting of the main ingredient of this soup. In my experience, the old adage about a nettle not stinging if you grasp it firmly is not necessarily true.

Ingredients

One very big onion
A pint of good vegetable stock
Four dessertspoons of fresh cream
Some salt

One tablespoon of butter
A big bunch of fresh nettles
Some mace

Method

After peeling, chop the onion finely and cook it gently in the butter till the pieces are transparent. Pour over the hot stock. Take your nettles (carefully) and wash and chop them before adding them to the soup. Cook for no more than a few moments and season with the salt and mace. Finally add the cream and serve with hot, crusty Norman Rarebit.This is a La Puce invention, and like all great culinary discoveries, results from a combination of necessity, inspiration, availability and serendipity. My wife is of Welsh descent, and has always knocked up a mean version of traditional cheese on toast, but this international variation has to be tasted to be appreciated, and gives the lie to foodies who claim you can't toast soft French cheeses.

Author's disclaimer (2). Be advised that, like the nettles, the cheese topping can gain deadly revenge if you bite too enthusiastically into the seething interior.

Ingredients for the Norman Rarebit

A stale French loaf (i.e. more than four hours old)
Some rounds of ripe (i.e. well past its official sell-by date) camembert cheese
Some garlic   Some olive oil

These are all the ingredients you will need for a Virgin Norman Rarebit. For the sweet'n'sour version, you are free to choose any flavour of jam or sweet topping. In my experience, marmalade, honey or lemon curd works equally well.

Method

Cut the bread into fairly thin slices (so it will be crunchy when toasted). Now surgically remove and discard* the top crust of the camembert, and slice the residue horizontally into rounds of about one third of an inch thick. When the bread has been toasted on either side, scrub one surface with a peeled segment of garlic, then drizzle some oil on top and rub it in. Now trim your circles of camembert into suitable shapes and position them so as to exactly cover each of the toasted bread slices. This is to prevent incineration when you re-toast the toast. Now it is time to pop your nascent Norman Rarebit beneath a very hot grill. Strange things will begin to happen as the cheese initially resists the flame, but you must hold your nerve until the soufflé syndrome takes over and the top begins to bubble and melt and rise. The trick is in the timing. When you think you have got it about right and the surface of the rarebit is nicely browned yet not burned, whip it from beneath the grill and liberally anoint with your choice of topping. The sensation of biting through the sweet crusty top into the bubbling cheese below is indescribable, especially if a particularly molten wodge sticks to the roof of your mouth.

* You can use the remainder of the cheese for all sorts of other purposes either culinary or DIY if your window frames need re-puttying

Main Course: La Puce Fry-Up (Lentil Croquettes with nettle sauce and mushroom *galettes*)

This is another fine example of using one's initiative and what's available in the larder to knock up an impromtu but interesting meal. As our guests claimed to be very strict vegetarians as well as reincarnated deities, it was important that the main course be meatless. Apart from being based on the fruits of our land, this instantly invented recipe also had the advantage of using up the remnants of the cheese from the Norman Rarebit, and got rid of a jar of mildewing lentils which had been sitting in the corner of the larder since we arrived at La Puce.

Ingredients and method for the croquettes

8 ounces of red lentils	One pint of water
4 ounces of fine breadcrumbs	2 tablespoons of peanut butter
A teaspoon of yeast extract	A little oil
A few drops of lemon juice	Some salt and pepper

4 ounces of cheese, grated (or in the case of gooey camembert, chopped as small as you can manage)

NB. For the coating, you will need a beaten egg and some more breadcrumbs, and for the sauce you will need some finely chopped nettle shoots and a standard white roux (see below).

After picking most of the stones out of the lentils, wash them, then bring to the boil. Add a teaspoon of oil at this stage as it will make the lentils softer and creamier, and help stop the water boiling over. Simmer the lentils for about twenty minutes till they are soft. Turn down the heat and beat the purée thoroughly to dry it out and make it even smoother. It will thicken as it cools. Remove from heat to cool. Now mix in the other ingredients (except the stuff for the coating and the sauce) and season to taste. Shape the mixture into about eight croquettes, dip them in the beaten egg and coat with breadcrumbs. Set aside to cool while you make up the sauce and stir in the nettles. While all this has been going on, you or someone else will have also made the mushroom pancakes, after which it will be time to fry the croquettes in a little oil for around five minutes on each side or until they are nicely crisp. Serve with the nettle sauce poured over.

Ingredients and method for the white sauce

Two ounces of butter	One tablespoon flour
Half pint milk	Some nutmeg, salt and pepper

Melt the butter in a small pan and while it is foaming, sprinkle the flour over. Cook this over a gentle heat for a few minutes, then pour the milk over, stirring well. Remember to go round the edges of the pan to mix in any of the uncooked roux. When all the milk is added, bring the sauce to the boil and then simmer for around five minutes. Add the chopped nettles at this stage, then season with a little nutmeg and the salt and pepper.

Mushroom *galettes*

Author's disclaimer (3). It is recommended that you use buckwheat or wholewheat flour for the galettes. It is not recommended that you use any mushrooms for the filling if you are not sure of their pedigree and edibility rating. In our case, the various fungi were harvested from the oak and beechwood roadside copse at La Puce by our dinner guests, and personally vetted by my wife before going in to the pan.

Ingredients and method for the filling

One pound of finely chopped wild mushrooms
Three tablespoons of finely chopped spring onions
One ounce of butter   Yet more nettles
Salt and pepper   A handful of garlic grass

Melt the butter in a large saucepan and cook the onions for a few moments. Add the mushrooms and cook for ten minutes in the uncovered pan, stirring regularly. At the last minute, add the finely chopped and tender nettle shoots and the chopped garlic grass. Remove the pan and strain the liquid for basting the pancakes. Put the cooked mixture into a bowl ready for filling the *galettes*.

Ingredients and method for the *galettes*

The French name for savoury pancakes, *galettes* made with buckwheat are a Breton speciality and have a distinctive, nutty flavour. They can be made in advance and stored in the fridge for several days, or even frozen for emergencies to wrap around a filling made with whatever leftovers are to hand.

To make around eight reasonably-sized buckwheat *galettes*, you will need:

A half pint of milk	A large egg
A pinch of salt	A teaspoon of oil
Two ounces of wholewheat flour	Two ounces of buckwheat flour

Put the flours and salt into a bowl. Beat together the egg, milk and oil, and pour gradually into the flours, stirring constantly until a smooth batter results. Cook your *galettes* just like pancakes.

Incan Afters: Chocolate chip cookies

On the occasion previously described, Mystic Peg insisted on preparing and cooking what she said was her signature dish, and a favourite treat 'back home' after she had personally introduced chocolate to the USA from Peru in her incarnation as an Incan High Priestess. As Donella had given our last morsel of Cadbury's Fruit and Nut to Cato that morning, I pointed out that they would have to be chocolate-less Chocolate Chip Cookies. Mystic Peg assured me that she carried her own supply of the vital ingredient, and though the dark little nuggets didn't taste like any chocolate I have tried before, the result was certainly interesting.

Ingredients (for about 30 small cookies)

4 ounces of butter	A half cup of white sugar
A half cup of brown sugar	One large egg
A half teaspoon of vanilla essence	One and a half cups of flour
A half cup of chopped walnuts	A half teaspoon of baking soda
A half cup of plain chocolate broken into bits	Some salt

Method

Preheat the oven to fairly hot. Beat the butter with a wooden spoon until it is creamy. Mix the sugars together, then gradually add to the butter, beating until the mixture is light and fluffy. Then beat in the egg and vanilla. Sift the flour, salt and soda into a bowl. Stir in the butter mixture until it forms a smooth batter. Now stir in the nuts and the chocolate chips. Drop teaspoon-sized dollops of the mixture on to a well-greased baking sheet or sheets, leaving an inch or so between each cookie. Bake in the oven for around 10-15 minutes. Cool on a wire rack until you can resist them no longer.

Drinks suggestions

With the nettle soup, thoughts inevitably turn towards a glass of Dandelion and Burdock, but perhaps a glass of cider might be more in keeping with the mood and location. (Or perhaps not!) For the Norman Rarebit, my idea would be a well-rounded and 'vigorous' red wine, perhaps a Côte d'Or or Chambolle Musigny. The interesting mixture of flavours to be found in the croquettes and lentils seems to me to deserve a full-flavoured wine like a good Côtes du Rhône. If you think the *galettes* need highlighting, perhaps an Anjou white Bonnezaux or something similar from the Loire would do the trick. It is a challenge to think of a wine to suit the cookies as we all know how the delicious darkness of chocolate mugs the palate. However, perhaps a really sweet Monbazillac or a lighter Montravel Rosette will complement and not compete.

Footnote

The morning after our encounter with Osiris and Ra-Atum, we woke up to find them gone and the following guide on how to live a full and contented life pinned to the porch door at the mill cottage. The note attached said that it was an ancient Tibetan mantra that Mystic Peg had written herself in a brief former incarnation as the Dalai Lama. Given the language and style, I have my doubts about its provenance according to Ra-Atum and Osiris. Regardless of its origins, it seemed to me to be a pretty worthwhile template for anyone wishing to pass through this world without damaging themselves or those they meet on the way, so I decided to take a leaf from the book of a fellow scribbler. The Ancient Greek author Diogenes was so impressed with the ideas of the philosopher Epicurus on how to find and hang on to happiness that he had them inscribed on a wall specially built in the centre of his local town. Lacking the skills and resources to do a proper job, I have framed and fixed a photocopy of Peg and Don's parting gift on the ruined gable end of the mill cottage. Though it later transpired that they obviously do not always follow their own advice, it doesn't, in my opinion, make the message any less worthy of consideration:

Take into account that great love and great achievements
involve great risk.

When you lose, don't lose the lesson.

Follow the three R's: Respect for self, Respect for others and
Responsibility for all your actions.

Remember that not getting what you want is sometimes a
wonderful stroke of luck.

Learn the rules so that you know how to break them properly.

Don't let a little dispute injure a great friendship.

When you realise you have made a mistake, take immediate
steps to correct it.

Spend some time alone.

Open your arms to change, but don't let go of your values.

Remember that silence is sometimes the best answer.

Live a good and honourable life. Then, when you get older and think back, you'll be able to enjoy it a second time.

Do all you can to create a tranquil, harmonious home. A loving atmosphere in your home is the foundation for your life.

In disagreements with loved ones, deal only with the current situation. Don't bring up the past.

Share your knowledge. It's a way to achieve immortality.

Be gentle with the earth.

Go somewhere you've never been before once a year.

Remember that the best relationship is one in which your love for each other exceeds your need for each other.

Judge your success by what you had to give up in order to achieve it.

Approach love and cooking with reckless abandon.

Travels without Victor

And low the mists of evening lie
And lightly skims the midge.

Sir John Betjeman

The year moves on, and all at La Puce is mists and mellow fruitfulness.

I don't know where Keats got the idea for his immortal line, but he would certainly have found no lack of inspiration here as autumn approaches. The days are still hot, but give way to cool and ghostly evenings as the water meadow becomes shrouded with a low-lying mist and the midges attract a squadron of dive-bombing birds. The full earth is preparing to give up its yearly bounty, and all the signs indicate a bumper harvest.

By the wooden bridge, the sloe berries look as if someone has coated them with layers of black paint and varnish, and they will add a tang to many a gallon of moonshine *calva* later this year.

Along the banks of the mill stream, a host of hazel nuts will see us and our lone squirrel comfortably through the winter months, and the branches of the giant beeches lining Hunter's Walk seem bowed with the sheer weight of their fruit.

Walking through the orchard, it is difficult to believe that such small trees could bear so many apples, and the figs and plumptious pears are ripe with promise. As usual, the old cherry tree has borne a thousand buds, but every tiny mouthful of brilliant red sweetness has been taken by feathered thieves. I have considered all sorts of deterrent from a giant hair net to a dummy eagle, but my wife says cherries are cheap in season, and the need of the birds is much greater than ours.

On the slope running from the farmhouse terrace to the mill

stream, my wife's vegetable garden is a jumble of colour and life as maize and brassica, late tomatoes and aubergines jostle for breathing room.

It will be a few years before even she can coax fruit from the new vineyard, but bright green shoots of life are already transforming the rows of withered sticks she planted just a couple of months ago. Even the deadly bramble patches are promising rich pickings for later in the year, and the tons of elderberries gently ripening along the miles of ancient hedgerows criss-crossing our land would satisfy the needs of an army of English winemakers.

But there is a downside to all this fecundity. Any day now, the first parties of local hunter-gatherers will arrive, and I shall have to grit my teeth and smile a welcome as they wander down the mill track to spend a pleasant afternoon plundering the richness of our woods, fields and hedges. Unlike their ancient right to publicly wash the family's dirty linen in our mill stream, the local people have no official entitlement to pick the wild fruits of La Puce, but it is a tradition established over centuries, and I long ago agreed to a compromise which would keep the peace.

When we first arrived, I spent many an interesting hour confronting total strangers raiding my waterways, woodland and fields; sometimes I would even find whole parties enjoying a barbecue picnic made up of my fish, fungi, fruit and nuts. On one occasion, a member of our rival community of St Jacques de Néhou arrived with a horse and cart so that he could stock up for the winter in a single visit.

After many heated exchanges and some near-physical confrontations, I appealed to our mayor for help before things got out of hand. He proposed I should agree to strictly local people helping themselves to moderate amounts of our uncultivated free food. In return, they would cease fishing in all ponds and streams, and not accidently mistake the contents of our vegetable garden as Nature's bounty. The rules of engagement would not, of course, apply to any trespassers from St Jacques de Néhou, who could be considered fair game for any man traps or other instruments of retribution I might wish to install.

The agreement has worked fairly well in recent years, and I have learned to show no overt animosity when stumbling upon a family halfway up a tree in Hunter's Walk or a young couple enjoying an outdoor encounter in the long grass surrounding the big pond. As long as our visitors do not frighten or deprive the animal residents of La Puce, Donella is content to see the natural bounty of our land put to good use, and secretly rather likes the idea of so many people sharing in the yearly feast that our small but fertile property yields up each year.

My enjoyment of this time of fruitfulness was, however, tempered this morning when my wife announced that Cato the werecat is a she not a he, and heavily pregnant.

Donella is obviously elated at the impending arrival of the litter, but I am not so sure it is good news. I cannot imagine what sort of mate would be ferocious enough to get within coupling distance of Cato, and because of the attentions of the local hunting clubs, I don't know of any other cats in our neighbourhood. I dread to think of the sort of unholy alliance which may have taken place, and what awful chimera may emerge when our werecat's term comes to an end.

*　　*　　*　　*　　*

Despite the pleasantness of our autumnal surroundings, I am beginning to feel more than a little stir-crazy. With Mr Bougie still awaiting the parts for Victor's operation, we have been virtually marooned at La Puce since Osiris and Ra-Atum gave us a lift home from the Bar Ghislaine. I am missing my mobility sorely, and have not been to a Jolly Boys Club meeting for more than a fortnight. During the weeks we have been without transport I have had to resort to cadging lifts from friends or passing strangers, but it is not a satisfactory arrangement. Apart from the indignity of standing in the road beside La Puce with my thumb in the air, it is not much fun being a helpless passenger with the average Norman driver.

Yesterday, Ivan the terrible driving instructor roared past the entrace to the mill track and screeched to a stop before I could lower my thumb. When he reversed back and offered me a lift, I had to pretend that I had been taking some artistic visual measurements before trimming the hedge, but I don't think he believed me, and screeched off huffily in a pungent cloud of exhaust smoke and scorched rubber.

Predictably, Donella is not at all concerned at the prospect of being completely cut off from humanity and civilisation for what could be months. We have, she says, more than enough vegetables, fruits and nuts in the natural larder at La Puce, and it is only a two mile walk to Madame Ghislaine's grocery store. People had to get by without cars in the countryside for centuries, and it certainly did them no harm. She is missing Victor, but obviously finds the prospect of recreating the life of an 18th-century countrywoman attractive.

For me, the idea is not so appealing, so I disappeared into the big shed this morning to look for the collection of bicycle parts that I have fished out of the mill pond over the years.

*   *   *   *   *

My experiment has not been a success.

After a hard morning trying to create one bicycle out of the rusting parts of a dozen, I emerged from my workshop with a composite machine which, like the curate's egg, was only good in parts, and lacked such refinements as a saddle, brakes and a left-footed pedal. But I was determined to attend today's JBC meeting, and setting off for Néhou in high spirits, got as far as our own roadside farmhouse before abandoning the journey.

It is a curious phenomenon that what looks like a slight rise from the comfort of a car seat immediately becomes a mountain when you are trying to peddle up it. We see regular streams of weekend enthusiasts sailing down the hill past La Puce with their arses in the air, but I can now see why bicycling is not a popular pastime with the local people, in spite of it being a free mode of transport. Then there is the personal safety factor; given the level of consideration shown by other road users to cyclists, I think I would be safer with Ivan the Terrible than on a bicycle on the main roads of the Cotentin. There are a couple of determined *cyclistes* in the village, but they are generally regarded as foolhardy adventurers. Our new resident Ronald Dedman also has a boneshaker in the front garden of his house, though seems to prefer abusing rather than riding it.

Looking it over recently, I noticed a woman's name painted along the crossbar and commented on the sentimental English trait of giving names to favourite inanimate objects. Somewhat bitterly, he corrected me, explaining that Valerie is the name of his former wife, and apart from the implied comment on her promiscuity by likening her to a bike, he gets some degree of revenge for her infidelity by leaving her namesake in the rain and generally ill-treating it when he is in a bad mood.

*   *   *   *   *

The transport problem has been temporarily solved, and I have fulfilled a long-held ambition. After the failed experiment with pedal power, I phoned Mr Bougie the car surgeon to ask how long it would be before Victor is back on his feet. The very good news is that the necessary parts will not have to be flown in from Sweden, but the bad news is that they are presently located in a remote part of the Lot, and will be another week in arriving. When I asked if this was the nearest Volvo spare parts depot, he explained that Victor is so old and his work so delicate that he had to scour France for an identical year and model to ensure a perfect match and lessen the risk of rejection. This, he said, will obviously increase the original estimate for the work, but give Victor a much better chance of survival.

While on the telephone I mentioned my continuing mobility problems, and he reminded me of his original offer concerning alternative rental transport. A deal was struck, and within the hour, he was chugging down the mill track at the wheel of the sort of combined tractor and seige engine one sees in grainy photographs and flickering footage of the harvest being brought in before the Great War.

After a session of trial runs in the big field, money changed hands, and I chauffeured Mr Bougie back to his home. Apart from giving me the freedom to go where I will, the leasing arrangement has completely changed my attitude to tractors and those who use them. Not only does the elevated position of the driving seat give a far better view of one's surroundings, but there is so much more time to reflect on life and its meaning when you are travelling at walking pace. For years, I have been used to sitting fuming behind other peoples' tractors, and been even more infuriated by their drivers' apparent indifference to anyone else on the road. Now I can see how easy it is to escape into a world of reflection and reverie, and forget about hand signals or keeping to the right side of the road. There is a definite feeling of moral superiority and even invincibility to be had at the helm of a sturdy piece of farm machinery in the middle of a narrow country lane. I am also learning some interesting new insults from other road users as they finally hurtle past, and as Mr Bougie said, I can now drive to the mill cottage by taking a short cut across the fields.

Although she pretends to be indifferent to my new toy, I know my wife is just as pleased with it as I, and we are now playing sudden-death rounds of *Happy Families* to see who will have the privilege of driving us to Néhou each day.

*   *   *   *   *

News of our former guests arrived this afternoon with a rare official visit from the local forces of law and order.

Claude the intemperate policeman called at La Puce on his way home from investigating a case of illegal *calva* production at a farmhouse near St-Sauveur-le-Vicomte, and had obviously been making exhaustive forensic tests on the evidence. We had to help him off his moped and into the cottage, and it took almost a pot of black coffee before he was in a fit state to tell us we had recently played host to a pair of master criminals.

Far from being reincarnations of a pair of high-ranking Egyptian deities, it seems that Mystic Peg and her partner are accomplished fraudsters. The couple have left a trail of bad debts and bouncing cheques across France, and conned hundreds of gullible people out of their money. The luxury mobile home had been rented for a week more than a year ago, and having changed the number plates the couple have been on a nationwide rampage. Their speciality is to turn up in rural locations posing as wealthy Americans, then persuade local people to invest in schemes which they claim will bring visitors and money to the area.

Earlier this year it was a dry ski slope in the Pyrenees, and last month they persuaded a whole commune in Gascony to buy shares in a theme park which would make Paris Disneyland look like a travelling funfair. Apparently, the crooked pair change their appearance and personas to suit the region they are working and the type of community they intend defrauding. Obviously, they made a fatal mistake in thinking that down-to-earth Normans would fall for their rubbish about a spiritual healing and meditation centre for Néhou. A bogus proposal for exporting illicit *calva* to the United States would have been a much more sensible scam.

Last month, Claude reports, the bogus duo were detained outside Mont St Michel by a quick-witted gendarme who heard them trying to sell the historic monument to a group of visiting Japanese. In the camper van, the authorities had found a map of the region with targets highlighted, and a copy of one of my books. Far from following a leyline to the village, they had arrived to seek me out, as they had somehow got the idea that I was a wealthy and eccentric author with no grip on reality, and therefore an easy victim for rich pickings. Unfortunately for them, said our friend while looking meaningfully at the *calva* bottle, they had not reckoned on my ability to see through their ruse.

Nodding modestly, I avoided my wife's eyes, topped up our local bobby's glass and decided it would not be a good idea to press charges for the recovery of the rainy-day money from our ornamental teapot.

When Claude had discharged himself of his official business, we spent a pleasant hour catching up on the gossip he picks up and passes on during his travels. From him, we learned that Postman Pat has had his operation and is in good shape, and strangely unconcerned about the removal of some of his most intimate parts.

Rumour has it that a moped belonging to a certain member of the commune has been seen regularly parked outside the family house in St Jacques, so an accommodation seems to have been reached. Nobody is happier than Patrice that, as Claude puts it, a suitable bull has been found to take over his duties. I refrained from saying that I am possibly even happier than Patrice, then gave Claude a bottle of scotch and an armful of posters advertising our flea market.

As he visits more bars than anyone else in the area during the course of his working week, we know that the flyers for the big day will be displayed to the best advantage.

*   *   *   *   *

My wife is triumphant. A friend in England has sent us a newspaper article which vindicates Donella's attitude to what she calls the modern obsessions with diet and unhealthily high hygiene levels. According to the report, a survey has shown that children who grow up on farms are three times less likely to suffer from asthma and all sorts of less serious illnesses. It seems that, rather than spreading diseases, constant exposure to a bit of honest dirt helps give them a degree of immunity to minor ailments. Living their lives in hermetically sealed houses with central heating and the hygiene standards of a modern operating theatre actually leaves children vulnerable to any bugs they encounter while away from their sterile environment.

Based on the report, my wife now proposes that we advertise real farm holidays for children from ultra-clean homes. At La Puce, the visitors would be encouraged to get their hands truly dirty, to handle animals and to generally get to grips with the realities of country living. Then, they would be sent home with a new attitude to life, and hopefully an increased resistance to minor illnesses.

While I agreed with her that the children of our commune are healthy enough, I felt bound to point out that, apart from the notable exception of a small number of village elders, the men in our area seem to die at a relatively young age when compared with those in Britain.

Smiling grimly, Donella said that this was obviously a vindication of the proper ways of nature in disposing of the male of the species when he has outlived his usefulness. Having fulfilled their obligations to father the next generation, most men just seemed to get in the way and speed their end by wasting good money on drinking and eating far too much. Given the laziness, dietary habits and alcoholic intake of some of the men in our village, it was not surprising that they passed on at a relatively early age and left the women to take a sensible approach to living a full, active and useful life.

Realising that her views on the subject were not likely to be changed by further philosophical debate, I left her to draw up some newspaper advertisements for working holidays at La Puce, and slunk off to the Bar Ghislaine to take comfort in unhealthy and solely male company.

*   *   *   *   *

We have spent the day getting ready for our combined car boot sale and market. The event will be staged in the top fields this weekend, and we are hoping for fine weather and a good turnout.

So far there has been much local interest in our flea market, but not a great deal of commitment, and a particular sticking point seems to be the charge of fifty francs per pitch. When I suggested the JBC subscribe to a club stand to attract new members, Old Pierrot said the last thing we want is new blood in our exclusive organisation, and besides, he could rent an entire field for a month at what I am asking for the use of a few square metres for a single day.

There has also been some confusion as to the concept of people getting together in a field to buy, sell or exchange unwanted household goods. As Mr Junot rhetorically asked, if people are trying to get rid of things they don't want, why would they expect them to appeal to someone else? More importantly, who but a fool would actually pay to take another person's rubbish?

Then there was the embarrassing interlude when a villager from St Jacques de Néhou arrived at the Bar Ghislaine and announced he had a whole load of items for sale at our market. Outside, I found that he had a pick-up truck piled high with old boots which he said their commune had collected when they heard that the people of St Georges de Néhou are so poor they need to have a sale of redundant footwear. Apart from the slur on our village, the incident showed that my literal translation of 'boot sale' on the posters had obviously not made the purpose of the event clear.

Anyway, as well as causing great offence, the alleged gift was worthless. When our visitor had driven off after leaving the contents of his truck on the pavement outside the Bar Ghislaine, I had a rummage round and found that amongst the collection of ancient footwear, there was not a single matching pair.

*   *   *   *   *

The gravest of news. We are in danger of losing our ponds and waterways and everything that lives in or on them.

I awoke this morning with the feeling that something was wrong. The day had dawned clear and bright, and the early morning chorus of birds calling for their breakfast was as loud as ever. Cato was in her usual place at the foot of the bed, regarding me with an unwinking stare as if challenging me to make a move towards her mistress. All else seemed perfectly normal, but I instinctively felt that something was awry.

Throwing on a dressing gown, I walked out of the mill cottage and stood, trying to identify what was so different about this sunny morning. In the distance, I could hear the occasional car racing by the top fields, and the World Service was broadcasting at full strength on our vineyard radio, but something was definitely missing; something that was so natural and constant to our everyday surroundings that I took it for granted.

Then I realised that I could not hear the water. One of the joys of our early days at La Puce was to wake to the music of the unending cascade pouring into the grotto, and nowadays the coursing of the waterways at La Puce is as much part of our lives as breathing, and so goes generally unnoticed.

Standing on the wooden bridge, I watched the miserable trickle dripping into the mill pond, then hurried to the grotto. Even though we have been through a relatively dry spell, the cascade should still have been discharging thousands of gallons a minute into the water basin, but now it was down to a sluggish flow. At the height of the severest drought, I had never seen it so low.

In the water meadow, I found only an insipid flow issuing from the pipes which channel water from the stream and in to our ponds. Although it must have been my imagination, the cairn of stones we recently built in the big pond seemed higher above the surface, and I saw one of Triple Salco's troupe of performing frogs crouched on the top, peering glumly at the water far below.

I stumbled on upstream to where our land gives way to a patchwork of small fields and the tiny but usually fast-flowing *Lude* comes on to our land, when the cause of the problem became immediately clear.

In recent weeks I had seen no further evidence of encroachment on our terrain by our mystery neighbour, so had assumed he had given up his territorial ambitions and consequently relaxed my vigilance. But ducking under the string of barbed wire and on to foreign territory, I saw where all our water was going.

Since my last visit to this end of our property, a huge pond has been dug in the middle of the field next to the water meadow, and is being fed through a pipe leading from a concrete dam sitting across *le Lude*. Some water is still finding its way around and over the barrier, but not enough to keep our ponds and waterways full. While we have been away mapping the attractions of the Cotentin, an unknown hand has diverted the life force of La Puce away from our land, and from the creatures who have need of it for their continued existence.

*   *   *   *   *

We have been to see a renowned and inevitably very expensive *notaire* in Cherbourg about our problem, and the news is not encouraging.

Like most lawyers I have dealt with over the years, he obviously charges a huge hourly rate for telling his customers what they already know. According to French law, he had said, there is nothing to stop our unknown neighbour from diverting some of our water into his new trout pond, as long as he pipes the overflow back to the original course of the stream. As this is not happening, we may take steps to force him to do so. What we have to do first is identify the mystery culprit and ask him officially and in front of witnesses to fulfil his responsibilities. This, as our specialist lawyer told us while speaking maddeningly slowly and trying not to look at an ornate carriage clock on his desk, may not be an easy task and will inevitably take time and the services of his expert team of researchers and legal executives. There will more than probably be many different owners of the strips of land surrounding our property. All should have registered their ownership, but some will have died and passed their land on, or come to an informal arrangement and sold the rights to use it to a second or even third party. Although the law is clearly on our side, it could take at least a month to identify the owner or owners of the trout pond and the land on which it has been built. Then, after the official request and warning, enforcement papers would be served if he, she or they do not comply with his, her or their responsibilities.

Sitting back in his chair and making a steeple of his hands

before peering at us over the top of his designer spectacles and obviously trying to refrain from licking his lips and appearing too gleeful, he said we should not worry; it might take a little time and money to sort out, but the laws of the land are on our side in this matter. He did not add that, France being France and unlike some other uncivilised countries, we can expect justice in spite of being foreigners, but it was in his eyes.

Leaving the office after paying for our legal representative's hot lunches for at least a fortnight, we sat glumly in a bar while waiting for the taxi and discussed our options, which did not take long.

As we know from experience, the French legal system is not renowned for its speed of due process. This is why most people prefer to avoid becoming involved in litigation which even if successful may cost them dear in time, frustration and money. Just recently in our region, a judge was shot dead on his doorstep by a plaintiff who disagreed with his decision in a trifling case. All we want is for our small stream to be returned to its rightful course, but even if we have our legal way, it could be too late for the residents of the waterways of La Puce.

As usual when we have an apparently insoluble rural problem, I decided to go to the elders of the Jolly Boys Club for counsel and advice. They of all people will not only know the letter of the law as it is applied in rural areas, but also how to get round it.

*   *   *   *   *

The emergency meeting with my friends in the JBC has taken place. Donella is in the water meadow checking if our longest hose will reach from the mill garden tap to the big pond. She also intends going through the telephone directory to see if there are any water diviners practicing in the area, but I do not think this service will be much in demand in the Cotentin. My wife is the strongest of women, but the loss of our little stream has affected

146

her deeply.

Taking her in my arms before she set out for her beloved waterways, I promised that her aquatic friends will not be left high and dry, whatever it takes to find a solution. In the meantime, we must hope for rain, and lots of it.

*   *   *   *   *

Our latest bulletin from friends elsewhere in France has provided some much needed light relief.

John and Lynn Carter have lived and worked for more than thirteen years in the Loire valley, and their company Properties in France specialises in nursing customers through every stage of the home-buying process.

Along with an interesting local recipe, Lynn Carter passes on a story about a couple who recently arrived on their doorstep in search of accommodation for the night. As their guest quarters were already full, Lynn recommended a good and reasonably priced hotel in the area, and, suitably grateful for her help and directions, the couple left.

Some time after midnight, they returned and asked for the use of the Carter's sofa, as they could get no response from the hotel in spite of standing at the door knocking for hours. What was so surprising, they said, was how modern, impressive and large the tower of glass and metal was, but lacking a single soul to book them in.

Not knowing of a hotel of that description in the area, Lynn asked for the name, and the couple explained that written large above the revolving entrance door were the words *Hôtel des Impôts.* It was then left to our friends to gently explain that the couple had spent their evening trying to book a room in the region's main tax office.

Carte des Carters

To start: *Petites Fritures*

As a bacon sandwich is a must-have snack for a British lorry-driver, this dish of deep-fried fish is a traditional favourite with and speciality of Loire mariners, and can still be found in many little cafés along the riverside. The perfect *fritures* should be made with small and very fresh fish, but fillets of larger white species qualify if they are cut into thin strips. These are then called 'goujonnettes' after *goujon*, the most common small fish in the Loire. In Britain, whitebait would probably be the fish of choice for this dish.

Ingredients (for four)

The best part of a kilo of your chosen fish
300 ml milk   200g seasoned flour
Some parsley   Some lemon

Method

Having washed and dried the fish or fillets, dip them in milk and then coat with flour. Heat your deep fat to very hot, then coat and fry your *goujons* or *goujonnettes* several times until they are brown and crispy. When you have fished the fish out, let the fat cool for a few minutes before frying the parsley for a few seconds. Garnish your fish dish with sprigs of parsley and lemon wedges.

The main course: *Noisettes de porc aux pruneaux*

Pruneaux de Tours is a renowned Loirean dish, but there is some confusion as to the origin of the name. Some say that the idea originated in the town of Tours, others that the *tours* bit actually refers to the towers in which fresh plums were dried for winter use.

Ingredients (for four)

A dozen prunes
Some cinnamon
30g flour
80ml *crème fraiche*

300ml dry white wine
750g boned pork loin
45g butter
A tablespoon of redcurrant jelly

Method

The night before you set to work, put the plums in the wine to soak. Next morning, drain them off, but keep the prune-flavoured wine. Stone the plums and replace them in the liquid with a pinch of cinnamon. Put in a pan and simmer until tender (usually about half an hour). Now prepare the *noisettes* part of the dish by rolling the pork and tying it off every inch or so. Then slice between the string, and season the little parcels. Flour them, then sauté the pork in butter for a few minutes on each side or until they are no longer pink in the middle. Drain the plums and add them to the pork slices on a serving plate and keep warm while you make the sauce. To do so, put the wine liquid in the pan and boil until it reduces, then add the cream and the redcurrant jelly. Spoon the sauce over the pork and serve.

Afters: *Quatre Quarts aux Fruits*

This is the French version of our pound cake, and the Loire speciality is to bake any of a variety of summer fruits in with the batter.

Ingredients (serves six)

180g flour
180g sugar
A few drops of vanilla essence

2 tsp baking powder
3 eggs
250g stoned fresh cherries

Method

Brush a ten-inch round cake tin with melted butter, then line just the base with buttered greaseproof paper. Sprinkle the tin lightly with sugar. When you have set the oven to a moderate heat (175°C/350°F), sift the flour with the baking powder and a pinch of salt. Now cream the butter in a bowl, add the sugar and beat the mixture for a few minutes till it is fluffy. Now add the eggs one at a time, beating well in between, and then beat in the vanilla flavouring. Fold the flour into the mixture in three batches. Now spoon half the batter into the lined cake tin, and arrange the fruit over the top before adding the rest of the batter mix. Simply knock out any air bubbles at this stage and bake in the oven for just over half an hour, or until your pound cake shrinks from the sides of the pan and the top springs back when you press it.

Now on to the drinks. To titillate the palate ready for the meal why not, as an aperitif, try a little Bouvet Laudabay Trésor Brut sparkling wine from Saumur? Then with the *fritures de la Loire*, a Muscadet sur Lie, for example Château de la Gravelle, Grande Cuvée Don Quichotte 1997 would go nicely with the fish.

With the pork, although a white meat, a firm favourite with us would be a Saumur Champigny. It is quite a light red, and best served slightly chilled. A 1997 Château Hureau is an excellent example, as is Domaine Filliatreau Vieilles Vignes 1998.

With the dessert, what better than one of the sweet white wines from the banks of the River Layon, south of Saumur? For example, a 1997 Château de Bois-Brinçon from Faye d'Anjou, a vineyard which dates back to 1219.

Finally, visitors wanting to finish their meal authentically should chat to the local farmers who, with a little persuasion, will produce an *eau de vie* distilled in the corner of an old barn from the locally grown William pears (*Eau de Vie Poires Williams*). To save any confusion they normally bottle this in Perrier bottles carefully conserved for the purpose! To get the best result, the trick is to pour a small quantity in the still- warm cups from which you have just drunk the thick black coffee. The aroma is wonderful!

Market forces

No profit grows where is no pleasure taken.

William Shakespeare

Just when we need rain so badly, we are languishing in an arid Indian summer.

The weather bodes well for tomorrow's flea market, but ill for our waterways and all those who live in and off them. The rainy season in the Cotentin often lasts all year, which is why the grass is so green and the ditches alongside the roads so deep and accommodating. But it has been a remarkably dry autumn, with no more than the odd shower since our unknown neighbour turned the tap off by building a barrier across his few yards of the river *Lude*. Today we are going on another expensive visit to the specialist lawyer in Cherbourg and my wife and I have fallen out over our mode of travel.

According to Mr Bougie, Victor the Volvo has had his operation and is on the road to recovery, but Donella has refused to take him out of convalescence until he is much stronger. I gave the tractor a polish this morning, but Donella had reservations about the effect of turning up in the car park of a swish solicitor's office at the wheel of an ancient earth-moving machine.

Eventually, I agreed to invest in another horrendously expensive taxi ride, as on reflection, appearing with our vintage tractor may not have the desired effect. Rather than inclining the *notaire* to keep his fees low as we are so obviously poor, the ruse might actually encourage him to inflate the bill because he thinks we are a pair of gullible country bumpkins.

*   *   *   *   *

As I thought, our journey to Cherbourg has been a complete waste of time and money. Our *notaire* clearly does not understand how concerned my wife is at the prospect of losing all the inhabitants of our stream, ponds and bogs.

The only time he expressed any interest was when I tried to explain how the threat to the delicate balance of our eco-chain could endanger not only the aquatic creatures, but the birds who live with and off them. When I talked about the larks, wrens and wagtails which visit us in great numbers to work the waterways at La Puce, he said he was extremely sympathetic for their potential loss, as he knew what good eating small and delicately boned birds can make.

On our way back to La Puce, I persuaded the taxi driver to take us to Old Pierrot's remote home in the Val de Néhou, and left him nervously watching our friend's sinisterly murmuring flock of crow familiars while we went in to ask for help.

Disappointingly for a man who claims such a long and intimate acquaintance with sorcery and white magic, our local immortal could not come up with a single spell or incantation to end the drought. As he said, the one thing that the Cotentin is not short of is rain, so the only ancient and effective ceremonies he has come across in the past centuries are those which stop rather than start a downpour.

*   *   *   *   *

Donella was briefly lifted from her mood of despondency when Victor came home to La Puce this afternoon. Though he should be perfectly fit to return to active service, my wife says he is merely on the start of the long road to recovery, and will not leave his resting place in the mill garden for some weeks to come. She has also ruled that, from now on, he must not be subjected to any abnormally heavy loads or long journeys. It is doubtful that I will ever be allowed to take the wheel or even sit in our family car again because of my weight and sometimes brutal driving techniques.

To be honest, I am not displeased, as this means I will be able to play with our tractor for a little while longer. Perhaps I will be able to make a deal with Mr Bougie to buy it outright. Yesterday, and just to try my hand at the controls of the earthmoving attachment, I made a start on digging a new pond in the water meadow. My wife said the exercise was pointless. If we do not regain the full flow of the *Lude*, we will have more than enough empty holes in the ground.

I know she fears the worst, but since the last meeting of the JBC I am hopeful that all will be resolved happily in the matter of our obdurate neighbour, and gaining more familiarity with the controls and capabilities of our sturdy tractor is a very necessary part of the plan.

* * * * *

Cato has gone into confinement, and I have been banished to the sofa in front of the wood-burning stove. Our expectant mother has chosen to give birth in the dark cupboard behind our bed, and so the upper floor is out of bounds until the arrival of her litter.

This is bad news for me, but even worse news for the mouse family, generations of whom have been living quietly in the attic for more than five years. With a pefectly straight face, Donella said the exclusion zone is for my own safety, as it is only natural that Cato will tend to become a little aggressive during her most vulnerable time. I just gave a hollow laugh and asked sarcastically if I could borrow my wife's silver earrings to fashion some special shotgun pellets. Actually, I am pleased with her current preoccupations. At least the distractions of the impending birth and nursing Victor back to health are helping keep her mind off what is happening to our waterways.

When I visited the big pond this morning I saw that the level is still falling, and dozens of burrow holes have been exposed above the murky surface. Apart from the crays, I suspect that many other residents have moved on, and there is now a definite air of desolation about the once-cheerful place.

The blocking of the *Lude* has reminded me just how rich with wildlife our land has become over the years, and how much I have come to enjoy the company of our host of regular visitors and residents. Together with Donella's almost mystical powers of attraction, our attitude of leaving things to nature and making La Puce a no-go area for hunters has encouraged an unusually wide variety of creatures to set up home or seek sanctuary with us.

In the air, larger species like herons, kestrels, buzzards, rooks and crows are daily callers, and smaller birds who make good use of the water meadow include wagtails, robins, finches, tits, swallows, swifts and our wren family, and, of course, the elusive local kingfisher who has chosen La Puce as his favourite fast-food outlet.

After dark the sky is still busy with owls, bats and nightjars arriving to dine and socialise. On the ground, moles, grass snakes, lizards, stag beetles, glow-worms hedgehogs, voles, field and harvest mice and shrews thrive beneath the natural cover of the waist-high grass.

When sitting quietly by the big pond, I have even seen the occasional pine marten, and just once, probably the last living grouse in all Cotentin. In a complicated world, it is very relaxing to sit and watch creatures who have no other day-to-day considerations but survival and procreation. Their life might seem pointless to many, but perhaps they are the lucky ones. They may have relatively low intelligence and emotional levels, but they don't have to worry about the meaning of life, paying the mortgage or fretting if their bums look big in a new dress.

Although I often complain about the time, energy and money my wife devotes to nurturing all these creatures of the earth, air and water and am even a little jealous of her affection for them, I know that La Puce would be a sadder if less expensive place were we to lose them. As my Irish granny used to say, it's a crying pity we don't know we're having a good time until it's over.

*   *   *   *   *

A day of feverish activity as we make our final preparations for the flea market. After much lobbying, I have managed to persuade a handful of traders to book spaces, but it has been at the cost of reducing the charge of a pitch to nothing.

Another part of the original plan was to make an extra profit by charging for the concession to sell food and drinks, but we have actually had to pay the hot sausage 'n' chip vendor from Bricquebec market to attend and add some credibility to the occasion.

By my reckoning and if all our traders turn up on the day, we shall have at least a dozen stalls selling a wide variety of goods. If enough free-spending customers come along and make the event even a partial success, the effort will have all been worthwhile and the flea market at La Puce will become a regular fixture. If not, we shall just have to think again about other ways of bringing in some much-needed supplemental income.

*   *   *   *   *

Seven am: Making an early start to the big day, it was with mixed emotions that I looked through the porch window and saw a cloudless sky. A year that arrived after such ferocious storms and flooding looks as if it is going to end with an uniquely dry spell. The best guess from our bemused local weather forecasters is that the drought will continue for at least another fortnight, which would be catastrophic for our waterways.

On route to the top fields, I saw that the ponds are now barely half-full. At the grotto, the cascade was down to a pitiful dribble, and the *Lude* is now more of a muddy ditch than a stream. It is the first time I can remember my boots not sinking ankle-deep into the boggy area around the middle pond at this time of year, and standing on the wooden bridge, I could actually see the bottom of the mill-pond and the rusting bones of the ancient bicycle parts I missed during my recent fishing session.

Ten am: The site is beginning to come alive as our traders move in and set out their pitches.

By the hedge next to the farmhouse, Didier has shrewdly picked a prime location by locating his cut-price electrical goods stall next to the temporary bar from which our intemperate policeman will be dispensing drinks and judging the home-brew *calva* contest. I think that my idea for this competition was inspired, and there is bound to be a lot of interest in who wins the best-in-show rosette. Claude has not bothered to take out a licence for the bar because, as he says, most of the products he will be selling will be unlicensed anyway, and it would only have meant a lot of unnecessary paperwork for us both.

Earlier, I offered to run a power cable from the farmhouse so that Didier would be able to demonstrate his variety of bargain vacuum cleaners, tumble dryers and hi-fi equipment in action, but he looked horrified and said the last thing he wanted was people actually testing the gear before they bought it.

Alongside Didier's stall, our local disc jockey has already set up his turntables and lights and is ready to fulfil his dual role as entertainer and announcer. To celebrate the occasion, Kid Néhou has been to Cherbourg to buy a new record for his collection, so visitors can look forward to a brand new selection of Golden Disco Hits of The Seventies.

Further afield, an indefatigably cheerful Morroccan has brought a feel of the bazaar to our fields with his colourful display of allegedly genuine ethnic clothing, leather goods and hand-made jewellery. I know that Sadiq buys most of his goods from Didier and that the hands that made the ethnic clothing and jewellery belong to factory workers in Taiwan rather than Tangiers, but they are none the less a bargain for that.

Next to Sadiq's stall, Ronald Dedman has put up a wallpaper pasting table from which he will be selling life insurance policies on behalf of a company based in Cherbourg. As he told me when he booked his space, it was his profession when he was alive, and few other people could be so well equipped to advise people on the best way to take steps to prepare for death and what lies beyond.

The hot sausage vendor is building up a satisfyingly appetizing ambience next to the main gate into the market, and beyond his pitch is my personal stall. It is piled high with damaged copies of my books at a bargain price, and I have pinned up a notice announcing that the famous author will be conducting a signing session at regular intervals during the afternoon. My wife is not optimistic that any of our friends and neighbours will rush to take advantage of the offer, though she admits that my works make very good firelighters.

But if my stall is likely to lack appeal, I have even less confidence in the prospects for hers, which mainly consists of an artful display of fruit, nuts and vegetables advertised as being fresh from the gardens and grounds at La Puce. The layout is very attractive, but I doubt she will do much business selling mushrooms, berries and nuts to people who regularly help themselves to the fruits of our land for free. Apples are hardly scarce at this time of year in our area, and I think her petition urging the mayor to declare the area a hunting as well as nuclear-free zone will not gain many signatures.

Adjacent to our family stalls is an empty pitch which was booked though not paid for by Osiris and Ra-Atum during our supper together last month. When I told them about the market and invited them to take a stand, they said it would be an ideal opportunity for Don to sell shares in the spiritual centre at the *Château du Lude.* At the same time, Mystic Peg would be telling fortunes and reading palms and cosmic auras at fifty francs a throw. When I learned they would not be at liberty to attend, I thought about putting up a sign declaring that our psychic friends were missing due to unforeseen circumstances, but my French is not up to making the old joke work.

As there will be no income from pitch rental, I have also set up a number of traditional English village fete games and sideshows, and among the attractions is a coconut shy with melons instead of coconuts, a lucky dip bran tub, a rat-down-the-drainpipe game and a mystery raffle. My wife does not know, but most of the prizes are cuddly new-born kittens of an unusual breed, and likely to make suitably ferocious guard dogs.

Noon: The big moment has arrived. I signal to Kid Néhou, who blows in his microphone for the umpteenth time, then invites Donella to mount the makeshift stage and declare the market open. The brief ceremony over, I cross to the roadside hedge and swing back the five-barred gate. The Great La Puce Flea Market and Boot Sale is now officially under way.

One pm: Things are going quite smoothly. The traders still outnumber the customers, but it is relatively early in the day. As none of the stallholders has paid for a pitch, at least they will not be able to complain about making a loss.

Obviously, my poster campaign has not been successful, and I am beginning to wish I had taken Didier's advice by advertising a football match to take place between the teams from St Jacques and St Georges de Néhou during the course of the market. That, as he said, would have guaranteed a huge turnout from both villages, all drawn to see the inevitable bloodshed.

In desperation, I consider taking the tractor round the local bars and supermarkets and paying people to attend just to keep the traders happy and create more of an atmosphere, but settle for leaving my wife to field the complaints while I make an excuse to slink down to the water meadow and check the water level in our ponds.

*   *   *   *   *

Four pm: If not exactly booming, business has certainly bucked up. School is out and swarms of children have persuaded their parents to take them to see the mad Englishman's garden party. As a result, the simple games and amusements are proving a hit.

161

There are queues waiting to take a swipe at one of my old socks as it is dropped down a length of drainpipe, but the main attraction has been my last-minute idea of making further use of our armoured tractor. For just five francs each, I have been taking trailerloads of children on an off-road adventure around the terrain, roaring through bramble patches and dense scrubland, across the uncharted areas of the bog, and then over a couple of sturdy planks bridging the *Lude* where it enters our land.

I would have thought the prospect of sitting on a tractor in a field would not have had much appeal in a rural area like ours, but children are obviously children wherever they live, and I think my chronic driving skills are adding to the frisson of danger that is vital for all white-knuckle rides.

Five pm: We have a situation on our hands. Predictably, the home-brew *calva* competition has proved the most popular attraction with the men visitors, and the inevitable male urge to lock horns has surfaced.

Earlier, a villager from St Jacques commented that I was driving the tractor like an English cook, and offered to show me how it should be done. To make matters worse, Ivan the terrible driving instructor took the bait on my behalf, and insisted on giving a demonstration of his skills. Half the men present then began boasting about their superior handling abilities, and things got quite ugly. With a flash of inspiration, I suggested that the best way to prove who is the best and most stylish tractor driver in the area would be to stage a contest. For a hundred francs apiece, competitors would have their chance to complete a circuit of some of the most difficult and challenging terrain at La Puce. Marshalls would be posted at regular intervals around the course, and my wife would be official starter and timer. The winner would be the entrant who negotiated all the obstacles with the least damage and in the fastest time. Apart from the glory, our champion would take the pot of entry money less, of course, my expenses for fuel and repairs to any damage sustained to the tractor, hedges and fences. Naturally, women would not be allowed to take part.

Fuelled by the *calva* and this challenge to their rural driving skills, more than a dozen entrants immediately put their names on the list, and the flea market at La Puce went immediately into profit.

Six pm: The situation could not be more tense. So far, eleven of the twelve competitors have traversed the course with varying degrees of success. I went first to establish the circuit and set a time to beat, and put up what was generally agreed to be a laughable performance.

The only contestant to do worse than me was, unsurprisingly, our local driving instructor. Ivan now owes me for one five-barred gate, a small oak tree and a replacement for Donella's vegetable stand, which he demolished before even starting the course after putting the tractor into reverse instead of forward.

Unfortunately for our community, the leader at this stage is a farmer who lives and works just outside St Jacques de Néhou, and is being claimed by our rival village as their champion. His land is even more undulating and overgrown than ours, so he is very experienced in the field of rough-riding, and acknowledged in the area as a complete *spécialiste*. I have also just learned from Mr Bougie that he is the original owner of my ancient tractor, so he has an unfair advantage anyway.

The only hope for our commune now is that the final competitor will beat his time and lack of penalty points, but this is a slim hope as the honour of Néhou now rests on the swaying shoulders of our intemperate policeman. Claude has probably drunk more *calva* than he has sold today, and his confidence obviously outstrips his natural abilities. He had to be helped into the bucket seat of the tractor by four strong men, and has already fallen asleep at the wheel twice. It is, however, in our favour that he of all the members of our commune is so experienced at handling a vehicle while unfit to walk, and the amount of drink he has absorbed has removed any vestige of caution.

163

After moving the women and children into a place of safety in the next field, Donella returns and discharges the shotgun to signal the start of the final circuit. This has the added benefit of waking our champion up, and having watched him roar off in the general direction of the course, I and a good friend sneak off to relieve the marshalls on duty at the bottom of Hunter's Walk.

Seven pm: The trials have had to be abandoned, the flea market is over and the purse has been won by our rival village. We have spent the last half hour treating Claude's minor wounds and towing the tractor back from the scene of the accident. The winner has taken his money and gone, along with most of the traders and spectators, but a most welcome visitor has finally returned to La Puce.

As we began to clear the site, the heavens opened and a downpour fell that was extreme even by Cotentin standards. The most likely explanation is that the elements were merely catching up on average precipitation levels for the month, but Old Pierrot has tried to steal the credit by saying he stumbled across a forgotten mediaeval rainmaking spell while going through his diary this morning, and had deliberately booked the downfall for the evening so our market day would not be spoiled.

Whatever the cause of the dramatic change in the weather, my wife is exultant and has been standing in her shirtsleeves in the top field, arms stretched to the heavens and tears mingling with the rain streaming down her face. She knows that the downpour will not solve our problems permanently, but says it will at least replenish our ponds and waterways, and perhaps even keep them alive until we can legally force our neighbour to do his duty.

* * * * *

Abandoning the clearing-up operation, we have squelched down the field and through the gate into the water meadow to watch the rain smashing on to the surface of the big pond. Then, above the drumming of the rain on the caravan roof, my wife hears an even louder roar. She looks at me, and I smile and nod confirmation as I take her hand and we dance crazily through the teeming rain to the source of the familiar and reassuring sound.

At the grotto, a foaming cascade of water is crashing into the stone basin to boil and churn in fury before fighting its way through the sluice gate and across our land on its journey to the sea. Donella is ecstatic, but obviously puzzled. Although a month's worth of rain has fallen in the last hour, the dam at the end of Hunter's Walk should be high enough to divert the strongest barrage.

We sit on the bench and I try to roll a cigarette in the rain as I tell her the good news. Thanks to Claude's drunken rampage, the dam is no more. Somehow, our boozy bobby was misdirected as he reached the crossing at the end of Hunter's Walk, and instead of returning through the top field, he ploughed our armoured tractor on to foreign soil and straight into the concrete dam. It was an unfortunate accident for which nobody is really to blame, but the accident was heaven-sent, as our friend's mishap has returned the clear, sweet waters of our stream to their rightful course.

My wife might not think much of my old tractor and our local representative of law and order, but together they have brought the life-giving waters back to our home and happy residents.

*   *   *   *   *

We are at the Bar Ghislaine, and I am splashing out to celebrate the return of the *Lude* to our land. We have also heard on the local grapevine that our neighbour has been told about the accident, and agreed to install a return pipe from his trout pond when and if he rebuilds his expensive dam. He knows that legal

165

action will be taken if he does not fulfil his obligations, and someone has told him that tractor races may well become a permanent feature at La Puce if he does not ensure we get our fair share of the stream.

Somehow, our local policeman is still on his feet, and has made it clear that there will be no official investigation into the incident. In the heat of the moment, he says, there was obviously some confusion as to the true path of the competition route and where my land stopped and my neighbour's began. These sort of accidents do happen, and especially in the countryside. In any case and as our local bobby points out while I recharge his glass, it is he who would have to make out any official report on the incident, and he is hardly likely to accuse himself of driving without due care and attention.

I order another round from Madame Ghislaine and return to the table where my wife has been given the signal honour of joining an official Jolly Boys Club meeting. Old Pierrot says it is to mark and celebrate the effectiveness of his rainmaking spell. More likely it is because she is holding the profits from the tractor rides and race.

Raising my glass in toast to our village, commune and all our friends, I catch René Ribet's eye and nod towards the door. It is time for me to show my gratitude for his help in suggesting a suitably simple yet cunning solution to our recent troubles.

As he says while we stand companionably side-by-side at the moonlit *pissoir*, when a complex problem arises in the countryside, who better to ask for help than a fox?

Epilogue

At the Mill of the Flea, all is once again *normale*.

Our little river is gurgling contentedly on its way through La Puce and to the distant sea, and the various ponds, basins and bogs are brimful with water and life. I have spent a pleasant day at home, and after clearing the roadside fields of the debris from our first and probably last flea market, I am enjoying a lazy afternoon sitting beside the big pond and reflecting on the passing of another year in our lives in this small corner of France.

Winter will soon be with us and most of our furred and feathered residents are making their own preparations for the hard times ahead. My wife will also be laying in stores to help them through the lean months, and this year there will be even more mouths to feed. Apart from Cato's huge litter, I have seen ominous signs at the waterside that, unless the Prince of Darkness has learned the trick of being in two places at the same time, he has found a mate. If nature takes its course, we could end up with a whole colony of ferocious muskrats. If this happens, Donella will be delighted, while I shall have to look upon the problem as an opportunity and talk to Dodgy Didier about the potential local appeal for bargain-buy and home cured fur coats.

Away from recent developments on the waterfront, Postman Patrice returned to duty today, and seems none the worse for his operation. In fact, there was a definite spring in his step as he delivered our mail and told me that it will be many a long month before Madame can expect the best of him.

From our latest batch of correspondence, I learned that Lord

Christopher has at last got his drawbridge in full working order, but has not been successful with the patent for his chain-mail underpants.

In the pleasant reaches of the Dordogne, Neville Palmer is still living a life rich in gastronomic adventure and philosophic observation, and our other settler friends around France are also enjoying their adopted regions and homeland.

Closer to home, I have heard from our inebriate policeman that Osiris and Ra-Atum will be spending some years of their current incarnations as guests of the Republic of France, while Ronald Dedman is enjoying his life after death in our little village, and still working on his plans for guided tours of the most interesting and lively cemeteries in the region.

Since the return of the life-giving waters to La Puce and the birth of Cato's litter, my wife has been in constant transports of delight, and I am relieved that the tiny and appealing creatures bear no obvious physical marks of the Beast about their persons.

The Jolly Boys Club will be in full session this evening, and it is, of course, my duty to put in an appearance. But for the moment I am content to while away another hour or two beside the big pond and consider how privileged I am when compared to so many people elsewhere.

Our daily life and small adventures at Néhou are of little importance in such a big world, and it is unlikely that I am destined to leave much of a mark on it. But I count myself lucky to have passed this particular way, and learned at least a little about the things that, to people like us, really matter.

The End

Other books in the La Puce saga

Home & Dry in France

Home & Dry in France follows the
early adventures of George and
Donella East as the innocents
abroad search for a home in
France, discover The Little
Jewel, and eventually arrive at
the Mill of the Flea.

**Home & Dry in France
by George East
ISBN: 0 9523635 0 X**

René & Me

The second book in the La Puce
saga, *René & Me* charts a
memorable year as our heroes
attempt to survive at the Mill of
the Flea with a series of bizarre
and doomed schemes. As plans
for staging metal-detecting
weekends to unearth the miller's
gold fall about their ears, René
Ribet moves on to their land and
in to their lives.

**René & Me by George East
ISBN: 0 9523635 1 8**

René & Me - the talking book!

Now you can enjoy the adventures of our innocents abroad and their ally the Fox of Cotentin almost anywhere!

This boxed set of two audio cassettes features more than four hours of readings from *René & Me*, complete with sound effects and special theme music.

René & Me talking book by George East
ISBN: 0 9523635 4 2

French Letters

In *French Letters*, the Easts continue their adventures in a land where time is cheap, good friends priceless, and reluctant tractors are brought to life on a frosty morning with a shot of moonshine brandy. During another eventful year at the Mill of the Flea, we encounter a new host of improbable characters and events.

French Letters by George East
ISBN: 0 9523635 2 6

"Quite simply, the best and funniest books about real life in real France I have ever read…"

La Puce Publications (UK): 87 Laburnum Grove, Portsmouth PO2 0HG
Telephone: (023) 92 678148
www.la-puce.co.uk